THE
PURPOSEFUL
WARRIOR

THE
PURPOSEFUL
WARRIOR

Standing Up for What's Right
When the Stakes Are High

Jocelyn Benson

THE OPEN FIELD ✦ PENGUIN LIFE

VIKING
An imprint of Penguin Random House LLC
1745 Broadway, New York, NY 10019
penguinrandomhouse.com

The Open Field/A Penguin Life Book

THE OPEN FIELD is a registered trademark of MOS Enterprises, Inc.

Designed by Alexis Farabaugh

LIBRARY OF CONGRESS CONTROL NUMBER: 2025001396
ISBN 9780593994207 (hardcover)
ISBN 9780593994214 (ebook)

Printed in the United States of America
1st Printing

The authorized representative in the EU for product safety and
compliance is Penguin Random House Ireland, Morrison Chambers,
32 Nassau Street, Dublin D02 YH68, Ireland, https://eu-contact.penguin.ie.

Dear Reader,

Years ago, these words attributed to Rumi found a place in my heart:

> *Out beyond ideas of*
> *wrongdoing and rightdoing,*
> *there is a field. I'll meet you there.*

Ever since, I've cultivated an image of what I call "the Open Field"—a place out beyond fear and shame, beyond judgment, loneliness, and expectation. A place that hosts the reunion of all creation. It's the hope of my soul to find my way there—and whenever I hear an insight or a practice that helps me on the path, I love nothing more than to share it with others.

That's why I've created The Open Field. My hope is to publish books that honor the most unifying truth in human life: We are all seeking the same things. We're all seeking dignity. We're all seeking joy. We're all seeking love and acceptance, seeking to be seen, to be safe. And there is no competition for these things we seek—because they are not material goods; they are spiritual gifts!

We can all give each other these gifts if we share what we know—what has lifted us up and moved us forward. That is our duty to one another—to help each other toward acceptance, toward peace, toward happiness—and my promise to you is that the books published under this imprint will be maps to the Open Field, written by guides who know the path and want to share it.

Each title will offer insights, inspiration, and guidance for moving beyond the fears, the judgments, and the masks we all wear. And when we take off the masks, guess what? We will see that we are the opposite of what we thought—we are each other.

We are all on our way to the Open Field. We are all helping one another along the path. I'll meet you there.

Love, Maria S

For Aiden

CONTENTS

FOREWORD

We all have a warrior inside of us. And it's our choice if, how, and when we want to put it into action and what we want to fight for.

Whether it's as a parent, caregiver, partner, friend, boss, employee, entrepreneur, public servant, or artist, we can get the most out of this short life by acknowledging and honing our warrior. When we embrace what ignites us individually, we can work better as a community to encourage each other to resist apathy, to refuse to let life happen to us, to not accept the unacceptable status quo. We can choose to fight for what is good and right in this world and have a positive impact on our lives and the lives around us.

This is what makes us purposeful warriors.

I first met my dear friend Jocelyn Benson in 2015 when I was performing in an off-Broadway play by Neil LaBute called *The Way We Get By* with my future husband, Thomas Sadoski. It's a story about how easily we try to silence that voice inside of us—that voice we fight to mute because it feels too scary or exhausting to listen to. The voice that threatens to break us open, throwing us off balance and inevitably changing the course of our lives for the better. That voice is loud in me these days and I'm no longer willing to quiet it—because of purposeful warriors like Jocelyn, a woman who fights every single day with integrity and intention for the people she loves and the country she wholeheartedly believes in. Nothing will stop her from breaking through barriers to ensure we all have the space, safety, and freedom to discover and nurture the warriors inside us all.

In her work I can see a country where we're more connected to ourselves and to each other. A country where our voices are heard in harmony. A society where we fight for each other and prosper, not one where we think only of ourselves and just get by.

Leading the purposeful life means learning how to speak our minds, ferociously stand up for ourselves, have each other's backs, call out bullies, and do all of that and more with courage and empathy. And it means that when we get angry about things—in our own lives or in the state of the world—we don't just stew about it. We channel that anger into productive, thoughtful action.

It's not easy to know how to do all of that. And that is why we need books like *The Purposeful Warrior* to help show us the way.

I am excited for you to read this book because you'll get to learn what I know about Jocelyn and her life as an honest, sincere, purposeful, happy warrior. You'll read about her work protecting the votes of Michigan citizens as their secretary of state and chief election officer and what that has meant to her as a mom, wife, and woman. The time when angry protesters who wanted to overturn a valid presidential election descended—with guns—on Jocelyn's home, screaming at her young child through bullhorns and calling her a "traitor" for simply defending Michigan's election results. You'll also read about how she (against our friendly advice!) ran a marathon while eight months pregnant, managed law school while her husband was serving in the US Army in Afghanistan, and, oh yeah, that time she went undercover investigating neo-Nazi extremists when she was nineteen years old.

And along the way you also get your own "how-to" guide on living your own remarkable, purposeful warrior life.

I truly believe that the future of our world will be decided by whether we in this moment can be there for each other, see each other, and unite our communities. Whoever we are, wherever we are, we can tackle problems large and small in a way that will support and create tools and innovations to make our world sustainable for our kids and our kids' kids. That is the world I want to create. It's one we all have to fight for together.

And we don't have to do it alone.

Amanda Seyfried,
actress, activist, and mom
New York, NY

Who Is the Purposeful Warrior?

*To be a warrior is to learn to be genuine
in every moment of your life.*

CHÖGYAM TRUNGPA[1]

Well, who's it going to be? You or me?"

It was 9:00 p.m. on Saturday, December 4, 2020. I was on the phone with Michigan Attorney General Dana Nessel. An hour earlier she had called with an alert: Police were expecting a group of armed protesters to show up outside the home of a female elected official that evening. We didn't know who. But as two of the highest-ranking female elected officials in the state, we knew it was likely going to be either her or me.

At 9:15 p.m. we had our answer.

It started with a faint noise in the distance. Then the chanting grew louder. I heard them approaching my home and felt a pit in my stomach.

"You're a murderer!" someone screamed into a bullhorn, loud enough to wake the entire neighborhood.

"Lock her up!" another voice shouted.

"Stop the steal! Stop the steal! Stop the steal!"

Over and over the chanting continued. I glanced over at my four-year-old son, Aiden, who was peacefully watching *How the Grinch Stole Christmas* in our living room while I decorated our Christmas tree, and then looked out our window.

There they were.

Dozens of armed individuals, some shadowy, others clear as day, standing just outside, ten, maybe twenty feet away from us. I called Attorney General Nessel.

"It's me," I told her. "They're coming for me."

I slowly set down the Christmas ornaments I was hanging and ushered my son upstairs.

"You're a traitor!" I heard someone cry. "Come outside!" screamed another. "Turn yourself in!" "You deserve to be in prison!" "Treason!" "Lock her up!"

I saw my neighbors peering outside their windows to see what was happening.

The shouts and chants reverberated up and down our residential street—obscene and graphic threats fueled by disproven claims of voter fraud in the 2020 presidential election.

My husband called neighborhood security, 911, and every law enforcement entity he could think of while I calmly carried Aiden to the bathroom and started running water for his bath, desperately hoping that would drown out the noise and maintain some sense of normalcy as the chaos unfolded outside.

Butterflies fluttered in my stomach, but on the surface I worked to project a serene, soothing demeanor. I didn't want my son to notice anything awry as I struggled internally with angst over whether the evening would create a lasting trauma for us.

Questions flooded my mind. Would these people attempt to enter my home? How many were armed? Would a stray bullet enter or ricochet into my son's bedroom? What were all the things I needed to do to protect him? How long until law enforcement arrived? What would happen when they did?

For the better part of an hour I made a dozen or so calls asking for protection from the state and local police while Attorney General Nessel did everything she could to get law enforcement to my home. As each minute passed, it was never lost on me that only one unarmed neighborhood security guard on our front porch stood between us and the growing crowd.

Finally, at about ten o'clock, Detroit police officers arrived. The crowd quickly dispersed. They were indeed armed, police officers confirmed when they arrived on the scene. But they were gone . . . for now.

That night was a harrowing exclamation point on a year filled with unprecedented developments, including a global pandemic, national lockdowns, and a highly contentious presidential election. But nothing prepared me for needing to shelter in my home and protect my family from an armed mob on our doorstep.

The crowd gathered outside my home with one goal: To scare me. To make me and my family cower in fear and intimidate me into succumbing to their demands and block the finalization and certification of accurate election results

Why? Because they falsely believed their preferred candidate, Donald Trump, had won the 2020 presidential election. And though results of that election—and 5.5 million votes of citizens in Michigan—said otherwise, the sitting president and his most ardent supporters refused to acknowledge they had lost that election. Instead they knowingly deceived and misled millions about the accuracy of those results.

But the truth, which I and others tried repeatedly to make clear, was that their candidate, President Donald Trump, had lost the 2020 presidential election. Period. No matter how much anyone might be upset about that, despite all the threats, lies, false accusations, and meritless lawsuits they threw my way, nothing was going to change that basic fact. Though he won the state in 2016, and would go on to win it again in 2024, in the 2020 presidential election, Trump lost Michigan. With that, he lost the electoral college. And with that, in 2020, he lost the presidency.

Still there I found myself, a full month after the November 2020 election, protecting myself and my family against a very real, immediate threat of violence—simply because of my commitment to protecting those accurate election results.

As Michigan's secretary of state and chief election officer, that was my job. Two years earlier I'd taken an oath to administer and protect the results of every legitimate, fair, secure election—without fear or favor, regardless of who won or lost. It was my sworn duty to protect the votes and voices of the 5.5 million citizens who had participated in that election—just as I would in any election, no matter the victor. Throughout my tenure I'd stayed true to that commitment, and I would continue to do so—even if the president of the United States himself threatened me with prison (he did). Even if a mob of armed protesters descended on my front porch, wrongly accusing me of "stealing" the election (they did).

It didn't matter. It didn't deter me. Defending democracy was my duty, my oath, my purpose. Just as it was for countless of Americans throughout our nation's history. Just as it would continue to be for all of us in the years ahead.

Now, that doesn't mean it was easy to hold fast to that purpose in the face of vitriolic threats. It was really hard, actually. And scary.

Yet it was precisely what many election administrators had to endure throughout that challenging election cycle of 2020.

Like me, countless men and women across America administer our nation's elections. We all share a deep commitment to doing that work professionally and fairly, ensuring democracy works for all. In 2020 we were locked in an intense battle over everything from how people were able to cast their ballots to how the votes were counted to the accuracy of the results. In every state, we'd administered a high turnout and secure election. Through it all we held our heads high and did our jobs with integrity because we cared about our communities, believed in democracy, and held fast to that fundamental promise in our Constitution: We, the people, choose and elect our leaders.

I wasn't the only one who endured violence, threats, and vitriol for staying true to my principles—and indeed we all as a nation saw just how far many would go to undermine the results of a free and fair election in Washington, DC, on January 6, 2021. That day we all watched in horror as a violent mob descended on the US Capitol in an effort to block the final certification of the nation's electoral college votes. But when it happened outside my home, a precursor to that tragedy that unfolded a month later in our nation's capital, it was just me, a mom trying to protect my family, who also happened to be an election official defending the results of a secure and accurate election.

It would have been easy in that moment to allow fear to overpower me. I could do little about the mob gathering outside my home, just as I was unable to stem the spread of lies that transformed into threats to our lives that entire year.

I felt trapped, overwhelmed, and powerless in the face of all that was transpiring.

But then I remembered a truth I'd leaned on throughout my life:

Despite everything around me that I might not be able to control, I would always have the power to define my next step.

I took a deep breath. My thoughts turned to those who had lived in previous contentious, noisy times, brave souls who had marched forward into the fire with purpose and determination. I was acutely aware of the risks borne throughout history, for example, by those working to stand guard over and protect our democratic process. People like John Lewis, who was a twenty-five-year-old student in 1965 when he stood at the foot of the Edmund Pettus Bridge in Selma, Alabama, facing down a sea of Alabama state troopers armed with billy clubs and tear gas, simply because he believed in the passage of a federal law guaranteeing voting rights for all. Lewis couldn't control the violence and the threats that would come his way that day, but he found power in his own mission: standing firm in defense of the right to vote. That was his goal, ensuring every US citizen had access to that constitutional right. And as a warrior for that purpose, he was emboldened to face down intimidating forces trying to deter him along the way.

I began to channel that same spirit Lewis and others must have felt at the foot of the Edmund Pettus bridge in March 1965. A fearlessness grounded in the truth that in a democracy the rule of law and the will of the voters must always rule the day. A power in knowing it was my responsibility, no matter how scared I might have felt in that moment, to stay true to my purpose and protect that constitutional guarantee.

That's when I realized: The people outside my home weren't protesting me. They were protesting what I, in my role as the state's chief election officer, personified: The will of the voters. Democracy itself. They wanted to nullify not my the authority but the voices, the votes, of every American citizen who cast a ballot in that election.

Voices and votes that were my job to protect.

My next step, suddenly, became clear. None of the incessant and graphic threats made against me would take me away from my purpose: Protecting every citizen's right to vote. Defending democracy.

As I locked into that power, connected to this purpose, I felt a surge of energy. A feeling of pride, and defiance, shot through me.

Clarity cut through the clouds of fear and anxiety.

And I knew: Threats would not deter me in my mission to guard every citizen's vote. They would instead embolden me to fight like a warrior to defend that guarantee with every breath I had.

The next morning, as local and national media started covering the story of what had happened outside my home the night before, I had one simple, clear message to everyone:

With these threats of violence, intimidation, and bullying, they are actually protesting—with a goal to undermine and silence—the will and voices of every voter in this state," I declared. "And their intention is to overturn and upend the results of an election that are clear and unequivocal.

But their efforts won't carry the day. Because our democracy is strong. The will of the people is clear. And I will stand up every day in my job for all voters, regardless of how they voted or who they voted for.

I have spent my career defending and protecting the right to vote of every eligible citizen. That commitment has never wavered, and it will not waver now. I will continue, as Michigan's secretary of state, proudly protecting and defending every voter and every vote.[2]

The Purposeful Warrior

Our beautiful, complicated, multifaceted history in America is filled with challenging and divisive eras. The year 2020 was one of those times. The emergence and spread of a deadly airborne virus and subsequent economic collapse, uprisings against the use of excessive force by police, the rise of domestic terrorism, and a loss of civility—it all upended our lives. Schools closed, grocery shopping became a scary task, air travel nearly ceased, and everyone sheltered in their homes, obliterating any sense of normalcy.

We all collectively lived with great fear, isolation, and anxiety. Norms transformed around us as misinformation flourished, creating a perfect environment for suspicions and lies to take hold. It wasn't hard in that moment for anyone—much less a sitting president—to convince people, even with all evidence to the contrary, that the presidential election had been stolen. And it was easy to vilify election administrators, like myself, as the thieves in chief.

There was just one problem: We were exactly the opposite.

Throughout the year, as the coronavirus took hold and a consequential election approached, we—like everyone else—were all fighting to keep ourselves and our loved ones healthy, to take care of our children as their schools closed, to figure out how to get essentials like toilet paper and hand sanitizer while figuring out which grocery stores were open, safe, and stocked.

On top of that, we were determined to make sure our elections were held on schedule, and that they went smoothly, safely, and securely for every citizen. In Michigan that meant working to modernize voter registration to ensure that every eligible citizen could register and vote from home. It involved sending absentee ballot request forms to every registered voter and installing over a thousand secure drop boxes across the state to give voters a safe and reliable option to return their ballots on time. And it required us to partner with dozens of nonpartisan organizations, including all four of Detroit's major professional sports teams, so that we could cut through the partisan rhetoric and ensure voters had the confidence and clarity they needed to exercise their right to vote.

Many of us did all this while being pushed into the spotlight and enduring intense scrutiny as the sitting US president and others sought to confuse citizens and obfuscate the voting process. Every call we made, email we sent, or decision we made subjected us to even greater suspicion, potential attacks, countless meritless lawsuits, and partisan investigations.

It was tough. It was noisy. It was a lot of fighting. None of us could rely on traditional structures or leaders to guide our way. We were facing brand-new challenges and had no precedent to rely on to help direct us. How could we keep poll workers and voters safe as a deadly airborne virus permeated every space? Where would we find enough paper for ballots during a global supply chain shortage? Who could we find to work elections, ensuring we had enough people to staff polling places and count ballots?

It still amazes me how we all rose to meet the moment. So many of us—Democrats, Republicans, and everyone in between—embraced the fight and got to work, innovating ideas and finding new partners to help solve our problems. Anheuser-Busch donated medically appropriate face masks, hand sanitizer, and other protections for poll workers and voters to protect their health. New vendors emerged with the capacity to print enough ballots for every county. LeBron James and other high profile athletes leveraged their significant influence to recruit a cadre of new election workers across the country. Military service members and veterans stepped up to educate citizens about how to protect themselves at the ballot box.

Where no previous examples existed to help us, we forged our own paths and built new plans to make sure voters could have the confidence that their democracy would be safe and their voices would be heard. We utilized data and the input of experts on both sides of the aisle to integrate multiple viewpoints and perspectives into our strategies. We held each other accountable, talked often and closely with those on the ground who were most affected by our decisions, protected our process from external political pressures or partisanship—including calls to cancel the election entirely—and gave voters certainty and clarity that their votes would count and our democracy would prevail.

When the polls closed on election night in November 2020, I was proud we had administered a smooth, seamless, secure election, in which more citizens voted—on both sides of the aisle—than ever before in our state.[3]

Industries across the country faced and overcame similar challenges as we endured a storm of crises throughout that year—health, economic, societal, political. In Michigan, while managing our elections, I worked alongside our state's governor and attorney general to make critical, consequential decisions in that fast-evolving, challenging, unprecedented environment. Each one required focus and resolve to guide our state through the storm on a battleship built with clear, foundational principles to inform every decision: inclusion, integrity, transparency, and courage.

Navigating those challenging times in what emerged as a consequential moment in history required us to be warriors with purpose. And our purpose was keeping people safe, healthy, engaged, and alive.

As the year went on, things got worse. The governor was subjected to a kidnapping attempt. Protesters showed up not only outside my home, but also at the Michigan state capitol, the homes of multiple other elected leaders, and even a convention center in Detroit where poll workers were working to count votes. We endured dozens of meritless lawsuits and a sham legislative hearing where Rudy Giuliani appeared as a star witness to try to discredit our elections and my leadership.

But all of those efforts failed. Our election results were certified. And the governor, attorney general, and I were reelected to office the following year by double-digit margins.

Through it all I learned that standing up for yourself—grounded in truth, the law, integrity, and justice—is not easy. It means fighting through a sea of chaos and challenges. It means dealing with stress and pitfalls and tragedy and turmoil.

But I also found—and experienced firsthand that entire year—that even in the most stressful, tumultuous times, a way through the rubble, the fear, and the chaos exists. It's a path that can lead us all toward a place of confidence, clarity, and certainty, emboldened with resilience, courage, and strength.

And that path can be found within all of us.

There were many times throughout my career when I—and any of the warriors whose stories are shared in the pages ahead—could have walked away, allowing the trials we endured to swallow us whole. I know a lot of us wanted to. I certainly did. In one year alone—2020—I found myself repeatedly, oddly, in the crosshairs of the president of the United States. I could have caved to his demands and those of others, even knowing they were wrong—either against the law or rooted in deception. It would have been so easy, so many times, to give in to the noise and give up.

But I knew that there is another way. Stories of warriors throughout history and resilient moments in my own life pointed toward that different path. An instinct and intuition in my gut gave me energy to persevere. The truth was on our side. We could use that to rise above the noise and chart a powerful course onward.

Instead of walking away, I found within me the determination and courage to stand my ground, face down the threats that sought to deter me from fulfilling my sworn duty, and protect our election's results.

And in doing so I realized the sea change of empowerment. Instead of feeling demoralized, I became invigorated with a newfound defiant boldness rooted in a mission that propelled me forward through the storm.

My job was to protect, preserve, and defend democracy.

I became a happy, joyful, purposeful warrior on the pathway to fulfilling that duty.

As I leaned in to that warrior spirit, a fresh energy illuminated my path forward. I felt like a fighter stepping into the arena. I found a renewed confidence in myself—a conviction that helped me find the words to respond to lies and vitriol with moral clarity. I was unafraid to push back and call out the threats against me and my family and election workers everywhere for what they really were: threats to the very fabric of our nation and to the promise that we live in a democracy where people have a right to choose their leaders. And every step I took in that direction delivered a feeling of joy—in standing up for my country, our democracy, and our Constitution. What an honor it was, I would tell my team, to guarantee that the will of the people in the 2020 presidential election would prevail.

Finding my strength as a purposeful warrior has helped me march forward through multiple storms and emerge successfully on the other side with my values and integrity intact. It's enabled me to succeed and, as Michigan's secretary of state, ensure that democracy prevails.

The concept of being a warrior evokes the image of someone with great physical prowess and mental toughness who's either defending their territory or going on the offense, running in to battle with focus and ferocity.

The purposeful warrior fights with that same spirit. As purposeful warriors, we combine the fearlessness and ferocity of a fighter with a focus on advancing a sincerely held purpose. We don't fight against someone, and there is no meanness or vitriol in our method. Instead we fight *for* something: our mission. We arm ourselves with the warrior ethos—that fierce determination to succeed combined with honor and devotion to our mission—and we direct that energy toward achieving a specific goal: a barrier to break, an intuition to follow, a benchmark to achieve.

Choosing to be a purposeful warrior helps us channel our passion and beliefs, unique and authentic to ourselves, into a powerful pathway that advances our ideals and values. It entails not accepting the world as given to you, the definitions others place on you, or the limits you worry might define you. Instead, you take your skills, talents, faith, and wherewithal and channel it all into aspirations that are entirely yours. And when you encounter the proverbial wind in your face that might deter you on your mission, you respond by redefining what's possible. The power of the warrior ethos allows you to embrace the fight and win it.

Each of us has within us the ability to be that purposeful warrior. It's a power that can light our way out of dark times and give us a sense of mission rooted in our highest ideals. And it's a spirit that empowers us to chart a path through stormy moments toward a more prosperous, safe, and peaceful future on the other side.

The trail is one that we must forge for ourselves, rooted in our perspectives, informed by our experiences, and guided by our values.

We find that path when we choose not to allow unfairness, injustice, and failure in our lives to dictate our future. It emerges when we refuse to allow things out of our control to dictate our own course of action or what we can achieve. It's about choosing not to allow events out of our control to define us or our communities—and instead, doing something about it.

Within you is the power, to quote Mary Oliver, to figure out exactly what you are going to do "with your one wild and precious life" and hold fast to your own ability to define what is possible.[4] And you must remember: You possess that power no matter what curveballs come your way, be they a global pandemic amid a contentious election cycle, an unhinged candidate for president, a contentious workplace, a toxic boss, or a bullying colleague.

As purposeful warriors we can rise above it all and hold tight to our own authority to build our own path—one that aligns with our values and aspirations. And we all have, within us, the power to navigate through even the stormiest of seas with confidence, clarity, and strength when we focus on what we're here to do.

Our job is to find that focus, that purpose, and then stand up and fight as warriors to further it—for ourselves, our communities, and our future.

What's Your Purpose?

Deciding to become purposeful warriors means looking around and within and thinking: Where do I see a wrong, and how can I make it better? It involves asking ourselves: What choices can I make and what actions can I take to ensure that our world is a little bit better as the result of my actions? How can I be the hero of my own story, and help others become the heroes of theirs?

It doesn't mean we have to have a grand plan for our lives. Your "purpose" as a warrior doesn't need to be curing cancer, defending democracy, inventing a new technology or form of communication. It doesn't even have to be a career, vocation, or job.

It simply entails finding a focus, something small or large you'd like to do, contribute to, or change, and moving forward with intention to further that focus. This mission can be broad and loosely defined, like resolving to further the common good rather than pursue individual or immediate gain, or doing something once a day to increase happiness and decrease suffering in those around you. Or it could be more specific, such as an action you take daily, like choosing to share a poem each morning with someone you love or spending one day a month volunteering to serve a home-cooked meal to individuals who are without a permanent home or living in poverty.

Your mission can evolve over time or remain constant through decades. Maybe you want to devote yourself to being present every day for your child so that they feel loved and safe. Parenting well can be a powerful purpose for a warrior. Or perhaps you hope to develop a new technology or launch an innovative product. Your work could entail keeping alive the legacy of an inspiring figure or ancestor, continuing their teachings, or helping to provide access to healthy food, clean air, or safe drinking water for everyone in your community, school, or workplace.

However you choose to define it, you have a contribution to make with your life. It is fully your own. It is a mission to fulfill with your time on earth, the heart of which can be found in tying your own values, beliefs, ideals, interests, and talents to the needs of those around you.

And then you fight to further that mission every day.

Even when it's difficult.

Because as a purposeful warrior, you don't let the world change you.

You are determined to change the world.

Through challenges, tragedies, and all the uncertainties of life, as purposeful warriors we ground ourselves in the power inside us to define our own future and forge our path in a way that reflects who we want to be and the impact we want to have in the world.

Becoming a Purposeful Warrior

This book may find you in a challenging moment, or one of uncertainty and change. Perhaps you feel you have something you want to change—a difficult job, a toxic relationship, or an uninspiring environment—but you feel powerless to do so. Maybe you have doubts about a partner, are fearful of criticism or ridicule that might follow a decision, or find yourself confused about how to handle a looming conflict.

So many things in life can conspire to make us feel like we are subject to external circumstances. We may feel our life is not our own, and that we are powerless to define our own existence.

The bottom line of embracing life as a purposeful warrior is that we reject that concept and instead know, with confidence, that we always have the spark within us to light our way forward. No matter where we find ourselves or how helpless we may feel, we can awaken the purposeful warrior that resides inside us and use that spirit to guide the way.

And indeed, we must.

In the pages ahead I'll show you the benefit of finding your strength as a purposeful warrior and how to harness it to propel you into a more powerful future. I'll share my own journey as a purposeful warrior—serving as a military spouse, waiting tables at an Italian chain restaurant, running a law school, investigating extremist terrorist cells, administering contentious presidential elections under a bright spotlight, and running marathons—in the hope of guiding you on your own path toward a meaningful, mission-driven fight of your own.

You'll also read stories of others who were empowered as purposeful warriors, like the women who refused to stay silent and led a national reckoning against misogyny by simply saying "me too," and the election officials who defied a sitting president as he tried to delegitimize their work, their voices, and their integrity. From entrepreneurs who left well-paying jobs to launch new businesses, sports leaders who built winning leagues through innovation and ingenuity, and everyday heroes who fought for a better world, we can see and be purposeful warriors in all walks of life. No matter our lane, industry, or example, we have one thing in common: Through trials and failures we seemingly can't control, we stay mission driven, resilient, and joyfully committed to our paths.

I hope that, reading these stories, you will discover how to chart your own course as a purposeful warrior—to raise your voice and take actions that serve your highest ideals. Recognizing our common humanity and intertwined fates, and fueled with a sense of pride and purpose, you can overcome challenging times, debilitating uncertainty, and divided perspectives and enter into a place of power.

That's the power of the purposeful warrior.

It's a pathway on which you can walk through life with purpose and passion, developing a series of experiences and perspectives that are uniquely yours. Focused on that mission, you can respond to your personal and collective trials in a way that reflects who you are, who you want to be, and the world you wish to inhabit. You can respond to fear and lies with courage, bolstered by truth and emboldened by grace and empathy. You can find the strength, resilience, and power—as an individual, as a leader, as part of a family, a business, or a nation—to venture out on paths unknown, into a future full of even more opportunity to prosper and flourish. You can build these paths so that, despite all that you cannot control, you transform any challenges that come your way into opportunities to become more powerful and strong—as a person, as a citizen, and as a member of a community.

And it all begins with your next step.

PART I

THE POWER OF THE PURPOSEFUL WARRIOR

Why we must stand up for others, call out bullies, raise our voices, and use grace and grit to make ourselves and our communities better.

Chapter 1

Everybody's Fight

Each time a man stands up for an ideal, or
acts to improve the lot of others, or strikes
out against injustice, he sends forth a tiny
ripple of hope, and . . . those ripples build a
current which can sweep down the mightiest
walls of oppression and resistance.

ROBERT F. KENNEDY[1]

Viola Liuzzo, a thirty-six-year-old white mother of five young children, couldn't look away as she watched searing footage on the nightly news of Alabama state troopers beating voting rights marchers at the foot of Selma's Edmund Pettus Bridge.

On March 7, 1965, during what became known as Bloody Sunday, Liuzzo watched as twenty-five-year-old John Lewis led hundreds of local voting rights activists across the bridge to begin a planned five-day march to the Alabama state capitol in Montgomery. At the foot of the bridge, Lewis and his fellow freedom fighters encountered Alabama state police. Under an order from Governor George Wallace, the police proceeded to attack the young activists with tear gas and billy clubs, causing severe injuries and halting the march. That night film of the violence was played on the evening news across the country, shocking many who had never seen firsthand such violence by a state against its citizens.

The footage horrified and galvanized Liuzzo to answer the call John Lewis sent out to the nation. She made plans to go to Selma the next weekend from her home in Detroit to be there for the second attempt to cross the bridge and proceed with the march.

"This is everybody's fight," she told her family.[2]

Liuzzo got into her Oldsmobile and drove fourteen hours through the night from Detroit to Selma.

She arrived the next morning to support those working to register voters and join in as they reattempted the five-day march from Selma to Montgomery. Their goal was to amplify the call for federal voting protections to Southern Black voters.

Viola Liuzzo was a mom, a nursing student, and a proud purposeful warrior. She went to Selma because she recognized that we are all our brothers'—and sisters'—keepers. She knew that we are all connected, and that we have a shared responsibility to each other and our greater world. Being a purposeful warrior helps us see our common humanity in that same way, and reminds us that if we neglect to see those connections, if we fail to recognize that our actions impact the lives and actions of others, then our communities deteriorate and we cannot flourish as individuals or as a society.

Liuzzo's story helps capture the first reason why you need to become a purposeful warrior: because we are all connected and our world—your world—needs you to step up, stand up, and engage.

Standing Up for Others

Everything we do has a ripple effect beyond ourselves. At the heart of being a purposeful warrior is seeing our connection to everyone else and the responsibility that comes with it. We are all inherently part of a larger ecosystem. The air we breathe, the water we drink, the food we consume, and the ways we travel from one place to another all serve to remind us that what we do impacts everyone around us. No matter how independent, isolated, or solitary we may feel, still, as families, neighbors, and coworkers, we all rise and fall together.

When we see our connectedness, we can see our duty to each other. But if we choose instead to disengage, isolate ourselves, look away, and refuse to recognize our connections, we become apathetic. That can lead us to discriminate, stereotype, and cut ourselves off from collaboration and community. It's nearly impossible to achieve any significant, long-lasting goal or prosper as individuals if we do not understand—and embrace—our connectedness.

Take, for example, the decline in civility and increase in divisiveness that has defined much of the past several years. The growth of social media and political divisions separated us more than ever before, causing many of us to lose sight of—or stop caring about—how our actions impact others around us. During the COVID-19 pandemic, millions lost their jobs, their health, their connections, even their lives, amid converging economic, social, and political crises. A lot of us dove further into isolation as we dealt with emerging and acute fears: of getting sick, of losing our jobs, of falling victim to violence, of being alone, of the unknown tomorrow.

And yet, as at so many other times throughout our history, in that moment we all still had the power to resolve to build a more prosperous future that reflects and finds strength in our inherent connectedness. In challenging times—which we may face as individuals, yet experience together—we can choose to resist falling into tribalism, division, and disarray. We can decide instead that we all deserve better. And recognize that in working together, we can all be better.

That is the power of purposeful warriors.

When we see and act upon our responsibility to each other, we, and the lives we touch, flourish. "Public good," Thomas Paine wrote, "is the good of all."[3]

Viola Liuzzo recognized that our fates are collective and intertwined. For her that meant showing up in Selma in response to injustices she witnessed, to engage in the fight for voting rights. She joined the march from Selma to Montgomery because she believed in her responsibility to be her brothers' keeper. Hers was a bold warrior move made in furtherance of a purpose: embracing Black Alabamians' fight as her own. It was not an easy choice, and it ultimately came at a great cost to her and to her loved ones. When she told her husband the battle they were witnessing over voting rights was "everybody's fight," she heeded the call for purposeful warriors to join that fight. That meant demanding their country live up to its founding, fundamental value: that we are all created equal, and that we are endowed with unalienable rights to life, liberty, and the pursuit of happiness.

"If you can meet deception [without] deceiving and follow in your heart a simple creed: be unto others as you'd have others be unto you," Viola privately wrote in a poem to her family while in Selma, "then nothing in all the world can hurt you, and soon you'll find that world is yours."[4]

When she got to Selma she was put to work welcoming, recruiting, and transporting volunteers and marchers to and from airports, bus terminals, and train stations. After the successful march culminated in a rally on the steps of the Alabama State Capitol, Viola offered to drive marchers who were exhausted from the heat and exertion of the sixty-mile trek back to Selma.

Then tragedy struck.

Viola was returning from the trip on Highway 80 with nineteen-year-old Leroy Moton when a car carrying four Klansmen—Collie Leroy Wilkins Jr., William Orville Eaton, Gary Thomas Rowe Jr., and Eugene Thomas—spied her and her Black male passenger. The men fired into the car, striking Liuzzo twice in the head and killing her instantly. Covered in her blood, Moton played dead, later testifying against the killers, three of whom were sentenced to ten years in prison.

Millions watched the footage of Bloody Sunday and heard Martin Luther King Jr.'s call to join him and others in Selma for the march. Most stayed safely at home.

Liuzzo did not. She responded to the call on her own terms, rejecting her husband's assertion that civil rights "isn't your fight." Overcoming the objections of those closest to her, she realized a purpose and impact far larger than herself. She could have remained on the sidelines but instead leaned in to collective struggle, choosing to run toward the fire, extinguisher in hand, when others ran from it.

In doing so, she sent a message of solidarity. The historian Donna Britt, who is Black, later reflected that "shockingly, Liuzzo had voluntarily put herself in a position where she could be attacked, even killed, for helping people who looked like my family and me—people she didn't even know. Her enormous sacrifice suggested there were people in this country far better than the newscasts suggested."[5]

And her actions preceded the enactment of the most significant and far-reaching national voting rights protections in American history. Five months after her death, US President Lyndon B. Johnson signed into law the Voting Rights Act of 1965.

"What happened in Selma is part of a far larger movement which reaches into every section and State of America," Johnson declared. "It is the effort of American Negroes to secure for themselves the full blessings of American life. Their cause must be our cause too. Because it is not just Negroes, but really it is all of us, who must overcome the crippling legacy of bigotry and injustice. And we shall overcome."[6]

Viola Liuzzo was neither a leader with great power nor a prominent figure with an influential platform. But she was a warrior who, as a wife, a mother, and a homemaker, in a moment of great consequence and with extraordinary courage, chose to stand up for her values and faith in a more just, fair society. Her actions were purposeful and focused, and reflected the person she sought to be—empowered and emboldened to act with a sense of duty to help her fellow citizens.

"If Mom saw a wrong, she took action," her daughter Mary recalled, recounting the time when, after a neighbor's house was destroyed by fire on Christmas Eve, her mother "pounded on the door of a toy store owner's home, insisting he open his shop so she could buy presents for the displaced family."[7]

Viola's sacrifice inspired a generation of voting rights advocates to continue her work to defend democracy. Including me. Her story taught me that, when we recognize our inherent connection to those around us, we can forge a vision for our lives that rightly recognizes others' struggles as our own.

Standing Up for Others Makes Us Stronger

Thirty-three years after Viola's fateful drive, I headed to Alabama too.

I went there to work for the Southern Poverty Law Center (SPLC), then the only nonprofit in the nation to vigorously track the activities of violent extremist groups. At that time, just a few years after anti-government terrorists conspired to bomb a federal building in Oklahoma City, our nation was merely on the cusp of learning about the deep network of terrorist cells within our own borders. The SPLC's research and tracking network helped supplement federal law enforcement's efforts to connect those who committed acts of terror to a broader ideological network so that they could seek justice on a wider scale.

Investigating these groups was tough, grueling, scary work. I was taking on a fight that was not necessarily "my own"—I knew no one directly who'd been killed or harmed in a hate crime—yet this battle against domestic terrorism was clearly "everybody's fight."

And doing this work didn't make me more afraid, cynical, or bitter. It made me brave, resilient, and courageous.

Because taking steps to further the common good and embrace others' struggles as our own doesn't just make the world around us better. It makes us better too.

My journey began a few months into my junior year in college, when I learned about Michael Schwerner, James Chaney, Andrew Goodman, Viola Liuzzo, Rev. James Reeb, Jimmie Lee Jackson, and so many others who lost their lives fighting for voting rights in the Deep South in the 1960s. And I learned of a memorial at the SPLC's headquarters in Montgomery, Alabama, that sought to tell their stories and pay tribute to those martyrs and heroes of equality.

I immediately made plans to visit the memorial in person during my spring break that year. My roommate and I flew to Atlanta and made the short drive to Montgomery to visit the memorial and the SPLC. While there, I met with staff and attorneys to hear about how they were working on the front lines to address racially biased hate crimes and teach the next generation of children to stand up to hate in all its forms.

I felt an urgent pull to work alongside them.

That meant taking a leap of faith and, after earning my college degree in political science, leaving the safety and comfort of New England college life to live in the Deep South, working a block away from the capitol steps where Jefferson Davis once swore an oath of office to serve as president of the Confederacy. Relocating to Alabama meant going against the wishes of my parents and the advice of my professors—all of whom hoped to see me follow a more traditional path toward law school and all the financial security and reputational pride that come with it.

I'll never forget calling my parents back home in Pennsylvania, letting them know I would be leaving behind the college they had worked to send me to, to instead live in an unfamiliar place where I knew absolutely no one. Oh, and I would be volunteering—as in, not being paid—to go undercover to track the activities of violent extremist organizations throughout the country.

"Where did I go wrong?" shouted my mother through the phone.

Yes, I told them. I was leaving all I knew to live in a place where I knew no one. And they shouldn't worry about my lack of income in my day job—I'd find a part-time job and work nights and weekends to pay my bills.

They were less than thrilled.

My grandparents loaned me their white 1985 Buick. And after classes ended for the year, I drove south.

It was a purposeful decision rooted in a desire to learn and work on behalf of issues I cared about—justice, equality, and access to the vote. I wanted to fight for people who had been left behind—by their government, their families, their communities. I wanted to learn how to be a warrior on behalf of everyone who deserved fairness and opportunity but—often because of the color of their skin—were met with low expectations, closed doors, and, in many cases, hate and disdain. I wanted to dig deep into our American history in a place that was at once the heart of the Confederacy and the birthplace of the civil rights movement.

It all made perfect sense to me. And it made no sense at all to my parents.

But like Liuzzo, in that moment I needed to defy my family's vision for my life and follow my own. It was a decision that meant moving to a new place where I would work with warriors who were filing lawsuits to seek justice in racially motivated hate crimes, developing curriculum to equip teachers with ways to teach about racial equity, and monitoring the activities of domestic terrorists. I was intentionally choosing to follow a purpose, an urge, to fight for something greater than myself, to understand the historic and modern-day quest to give every person a chance to succeed and prosper in our country. And getting there required that I stand up for myself, to my parents, in defense of who I was at twenty and the purpose I hoped to serve in my life.

It was a leap of faith. It was terrifying.

And taking the leap made me bolder than I'd ever been before.

As I made plans to relocate, all I knew that awaited me on the other side was an unpaid internship at an organization whose mission I believed in. The work was unfamiliar, the culture different than any I'd experienced. I knew not a single person in Montgomery. I had never lived below the Mason-Dixon Line.

The path was foggy and solitary. I was filled with a lot of fear and doubt. I felt completely alone. Where would I live? Would I be safe? Would I be able to find a part-time job waiting tables in a local restaurant, as I'd told my parents I would? And would any of these risks I was taking be worth it?

I didn't know.

But I drove south anyway.

Because more than a job title or a certain income, I wanted to build a life with purpose. I hoped to have an impact on advancing the greater good. I recognized our common humanity and the need to ensure we all live in a country in which everyone has a fair shot—to vote, to live, to work, and to thrive. Imbued with the courage of Viola Liuzzo and feeling a call to continue her legacy, I wanted to be doing the work she'd have taken on had she lived. I prayed to be someone who would choose to stand at the foot of the Edmund Pettus Bridge and march forward to further a cause that I believed in—in this case, seeking a world where legal rights and freedoms are protected for all Americans. And I didn't want fear—of the unknown, of failure, of loneliness—to hold me back from that fight and the purposeful path I felt called to follow.

When I arrived in Alabama I was immediately assigned to support the research department within the SPLC that tracked the activity of domestic terrorist groups across the country.[8] I was tasked with researching the online activity of leaders espousing white supremacist, neo-Nazi, and anti-government rhetoric, preparing reports for attorneys and investigators to help connect the dots when crimes occurred. My job was to find links between individual perpetrators of crimes and the leaders of terrorist groups who enabled those crimes through their hateful rhetoric and planning.

I threw myself into the research, writing memos to analyze and illuminate the lives, backgrounds, and motivations of various white supremacist and neo-Nazi leaders—some known, some obscure—who were, in the late 1990s, seeking to organize extremist movements and commit violent, hateful acts.

It wasn't long before I was sent into the field.

There I was, just shy of twenty years old, posing as a freelance journalist, meeting with leaders and members of hate groups to gather information on their activities and plans. I attended rallies and meetings, collecting and writing stories for the SPLC's *Intelligence Report*. I uncovered the identities and activities of neo-Nazis, delved into the motivations of women who were drawn to extremism through their boyfriends and husbands, and spent hours directly interviewing dozens of leaders and members of organized hate groups.

My first trip took me to Spartanburg, South Carolina. I spent the day interviewing Davis Wolfgang Hawke, the leader of a group called the Knights of Freedom. Operating under the pseudonym "Bo Decker," Hawke was planning a rally on a local college campus. He was a bombastic "aspiring Hitler" (his words) who, I discovered through my research, had changed his name to Hawke years earlier to mask his Jewish heritage (his birth name was Andrew Greenbaum).

"The Jews are trying to kill us, and therefore we hate them," he explained to me in front of a world map that depicted his plans, membership, and ideology. "It's just that simple."

I spent hours with Hawke, listening to and documenting his plans, all the while wondering if and when he would discover my own real identity as an undercover investigator for a prominent civil rights think tank. Those worries escalated when I returned to my hotel room that evening. Alone in the small South Carolinian Red Roof Inn, I sat reviewing the events of the day, all the heinous statements and plans Hawke had shared, terrified that at any moment I'd hear a knock on my door and he'd appear, there to commit one of those heinous acts against me.

I lay there in my hotel bed, awake for hours, afraid to fall asleep. I jumped at every shadow. Feelings of fear, anxiety, and trepidation coursed through me.

After a few hours of trembling nonstop, I realized I had to make a decision. Was I going to lie there and be afraid all night, thinking about all the terrible things that could happen if bad guys showed up at my doorstep? Or was I instead going to focus on thinking about how the information I had gathered that day had the potential to take down this brazen and openly neo-Nazi leader? A leader of a group that at the time had over a hundred members, all organizing to, in Hawke's words, "ferret out the race traitors" and "kill all the Jews."

I could allow myself to be consumed with fear. Or I could shift my thoughts toward what I was trying to do and find power in my purpose.

I chose to do the latter. I allowed my fears some space in my psyche, then set them aside to focus on the task at hand. Directing my thoughts and energy toward the work, I focused on the reason I was there. My purpose, through all the risk, was to collect information on an emerging extremist group and the hateful crimes it was planning. The task in front of me was to write a report documenting the information I had gathered that day.

I sifted through my notes and started to write. Slowly, the nervousness I'd felt was replaced with a sense of confidence and strength.

The article I drafted that night exposed "Bo Decker's" plans and ideology, and the danger he and his followers presented to the country.[9] It ended up halting a lot of his plans to commit crimes. And it ultimately brought about the demise of the group, and of Hawke's influence in extremism.

It also taught me the power of overcoming trepidation and finding the courage to let your purpose lead the way.

In the four years that followed, I continued to investigate hate groups around the globe, finding myself more confident each time and with a clearer sense of purpose with each new assignment. I ultimately spent two years working with the SPLC to expose domestic terrorist cells, and two more taking this research to an international level as a graduate student at the University of Oxford. With every story and investigation, I found a renewed sense of energy and confidence, rooted in the purpose of my work.

And I developed a deep understanding of the ways that extremist rhetoric and ideology lead to actual violence directed at individuals, communities, and, sometimes, entire nations.

That understanding prepared me for what I would later face overseeing the 2020 presidential election—that there is a direct link from the violent rhetoric of leaders to the hateful acts of their followers. Recognizing the links—and I saw them both at the SPLC in 1999 and again as Michigan's chief election officer in 2020—can help us better protect ourselves, our families, and our communities.

It was also in Alabama where I saw firsthand the multigenerational impact of slavery, inequality, and structural racism. As I spent time with people who had worked in the 1950s and '60s for a more just and equal world, I heard stories, over dinners and lunches, about the work and sacrifices of people who were part of that movement.

Those experiences instilled in me a deep sense of responsibility and purpose to further the legacy of those foot soldiers who worked and marched and bled in Selma and elsewhere to make sure that the one-person, one-vote promise in our Constitution is a reality for everyone.

That's how going to Alabama to fight for others made me a better warrior. I found power in linking a purpose to actions that furthered that mission. And I discovered the strength that comes in fighting battles not only for yourself but on behalf of others as well.

All of it helped me realize that I wanted to engage in a broader fight beyond working to take down domestic terrorist cells, one that could help ensure every person in America had an opportunity to fulfill their potential. Like the experience of my parents, who devoted their careers as special education teachers to fighting for their students to have access to a quality education, my time in the South exposed me to the depth of intergenerational poverty and my duty to try to help eradicate it.

In Alabama I forged a new purpose: to make certain that our government enables everyone to have a fair shot to succeed. From the lessons of the leaders and foot soldiers of the civil rights movement—from Dr. King and Rosa Parks to Viola Liuzzo and Jimmie Lee Jackson—I was instilled with a deep responsibility to continue the fight to ensure someone's zip code doesn't determine the quality of their schooling, health care, or physical safety. I wanted to help build a future for our country where inequality is eliminated and to create a transformational legacy that lasts for generations.

I began to realize what being a warrior for all those things throughout my life might entail. I saw how bad policies promoted—or created—structural inequality and studied the work others had done to try to eradicate them. Beyond policy reforms, though, I began to see the power of embracing others' fights as our own and standing in solidarity with others who are struggling. Conducting undercover investigations, researching injustices, and writing about my findings deepened my understanding of the purposeful path I wanted to pursue to improve the lives of others around me. It gave me courage to stand up for myself and endure fearful scenarios on the pathway to accomplishing my goal.

It also helped me develop a sharper sense of myself and what I wanted to do with my life. I was no longer a college graduate aspiring to a particular position or title. I was now less concerned with praise, approval, and wealth, instead focused on building courage, following my heart, and leading with integrity.

The Ripple Effect

Whether we like it or not, our lives have an impact on those around us. Our individual choices shape and dictate our collective future. We can ignore that reality or we can embrace it and move forward with an intention to build the lives we wish to live while serving as architects of the world we wish to inhabit.

When you choose to embrace your ideals, you'll find there is a ripple effect on those around you. As you stand up for others and embrace their fights as your own, you inspire others to follow suit.

The way Viola Liuzzo's story did for me.

Even if we don't intend for our actions to influence others' decisions, even when we claim to not care about an impact beyond ourselves, our actions, choices, and lives ripple outward beyond us. They are re-flected in our children—or in others' children—who watch, absorb, reflect on, and react to what they see around them. They are reflected in our co-workers, our families, our communities.

I've seen this play out as a parent of a young child. As parents, we know our kids model their behavior after us. When a parent serves as a purposeful warrior, they gain the courage to stand up for others too.

Two years after that night when an angry mob gathered outside my home, my son Aiden picked up a stick in our driveway and turned to me. "Don't worry, Mom," he said, referring to the armed men and women who'd gathered outside our home, "if the bad guys come again I'll get them with this."

He was six years old at the time.

In that moment I was instantly moved not just by his clear sense of the danger that had surrounded us in December 2020, but also by his decision to face that fear with bravery and a determination to protect his family. I asked him a few days later why he picked up that stick and started thinking about how to protect his mom from "the bad guys." He said, "Because you and Dad stand up to the bad guys all the time, Mom. I want to do that too."

By watching his dad and me stand up for democracy, our coun-try, and our home, young Aiden had learned the importance of stand-ing up for his family, and his home as well. Our courage gave him courage.

We see reminders of the ripple effect of our actions every day. There are the immediate people around you, in your family, your workplace, your community. From your mood to your words to your choices, what you do affects all of them. If we recognize this connectedness and embrace others' fights as our own, we implicitly encourage those around us to do the same.

Go to your child's school and donate items to make their classroom brighter or better supplied, and you'll not only see other parents follow suit, you might also see improved outcomes in the behavior of educators and students in reaction to the presence of a strong parental support system around them. Stand up for someone else in your workplace who is being treated unfairly, even if you have no skin in the game, and notice how that leads others to do the same in a way that creates a culture of trust and support among your coworkers and a healthier work environment overall. Start a small business, invest in someone else's, or help grow a charity in your community. Others will be inspired to do the same.

All of this captures the power of the purposeful warrior: working toward our personal ideals, recognizing our connection to all that surrounds us, and then embracing a greater responsibility to the common good. Doing so gives us the ability to overcome whatever obstacles life throws at us and see that the lives we build and the impact we make aligns with our vision and values.

Working for the common good makes us stronger and more resilient as individuals and as communities. Our families, loved ones, friends, and co-workers who witness our strength and power become stronger and more resilient alongside us. Our neighborhoods grow healthier and more prosperous, and our nation evolves one step closer to fulfilling the hopes and promises of those who founded it.

When we step up and engage, taking on others' fights as our own, we flourish and thrive. Together.

Chapter 2

Going Rogue

Never be afraid to raise your voice for honesty
and truth and compassion against injustice and
lying and greed. If people all over the world . . .
would do this, it would change the earth.

WILLIAM FAULKNER[1]

I was not prepared for what I woke up to on May 20, 2020.

Then I looked at my phone.

The president of the United States was personally attacking me on social media.

Me, a little-known state election official in Michigan. I was an obscure, innocent professional trying to keep my head down and do my job overseeing our state's election process, judiciously and without fear or favor. And then, in the middle of the night, the most powerful individual in the free world decides to falsely accuse me of "voter fraud" on social media.

"Breaking: Michigan sends absentee ballots to 7.7 million people ahead of Primaries and the General Election. This was done illegally and without authorization by a rogue Secretary of State. I will ask to hold up funding to Michigan if they want to go down this Voter Fraud path!"

Donald J. Trump ✔
@realDonaldTrump

Breaking: Michigan sends absentee ballots to 7.7 million people ahead of Primaries and the General Election. This was done illegally and without authorization by a rogue Secretary of State. I will ask to hold up funding to Michigan if they want to go down this Voter Fraud path!..

7:51 AM · 5/20/20 · Twitter for iPhone

Of course he didn't say my name. That would humanize me and make it more difficult to slander me. Instead, across the country, he was trying to make me known as Michigan's "rogue Secretary of State."

There was only one problem.

He was lying.

First, I did not send out absentee ballots to 7.7 million people.

Second, I wasn't acting "rogue" or independently. I, like many Republican and Democratic state election officials in May 2020, two months into the COVID-19 pandemic, sent basic public information and instructions on how to vote from home ahead of the general election that November.

Not ballots. Just information about how to vote from home in that year's election.

Not rogue. Doing exactly what my colleagues in Iowa, West Virginia, Georgia, and Minnesota had already done that month.

Not illegal. Sending information about voting from home, a right that all Michiganders have in our state constitution, is well within my authority as the state's chief election official.[2] Every Michigan voter has a constitutional right to vote absentee, and in the middle of a pandemic voters were increasingly reluctant to vote in person. I had a duty to make sure every citizen was informed on how to request to vote absentee in the upcoming 2020 election.

No matter where they lived. No matter who they voted for. Everyone deserved equal access to that information. So we sent it to everyone.

As I read and reread President Trump's post, I scanned the hundreds of hateful threats in the comments below it. How fast a lie travels, I thought, remembering the old adage, before the truth can even put its shoes on.

So now what do I do? I said to myself. Do I respond back, return fire on social media, correcting the president's lies? Do I call him out for his attempt to dehumanize me, letting him know I had a name and was an actual person?

Doing so would undoubtedly unleash more attacks—from him, from his followers, from trolls—and amplify his lies. Did I really want to do that? Did I want to risk the blowback, the noise, and all that came with it?

In truth, all I wanted to do in that moment was crawl back under the covers and wish I'd never looked at my phone.

Because, let's face it, it's a weird thing when the leader of the free world wakes up in the middle of the night and decides to go on social media to throw stones at a state election official.

When I was growing up, a letter or any recognition from the president of the United States—regardless of who it was or what party they belonged to—was an honor. Something to be proud of, to frame and hang on your wall. Something to tell your family about.

And yet. Here I was, looking at a message from the president of the United States *to me*, delivered on a social media app directly to my phone, falsely accusing me of something I didn't do and threatening to withhold federal funding to *the entire state of Michigan* as a result.

At first, I wanted to keep my head down and just get back to work. Maybe if I didn't say or do anything, I thought, people would forget about it and it would all go away.

But I also knew that I am not someone who sticks my head in the sand hoping that things will just "go away." I don't ignore bullies. I don't throw punches, but I'm not someone who backs down from a fight. Because if I, someone with a smaller platform and so much less power than him, didn't respond and try to hold him to account, his lies would threaten to redefine my reality.

I couldn't let that happen. I wanted to stand up for myself and for Michigan. This was a moment when I needed to speak the truth and hold a powerful person—indeed, the country's most powerful person—to account.

So I took action.

I got out of bed, typed out my response, and hit send.

And then hopped back in, pulling my covers over my head.

My response was simple. Factual. No one needed to help me word-smith or figure out how to say what I needed to say. I corrected the president, pointing out that I had not, as he'd alleged, mailed ballots to every voter in our state. In actuality I'd sent Michigan voters information on how to cast their vote from home in the upcoming elections—just as so many of my Republican and Democratic counterparts in neighboring states had recently done.

"Hi!" I wrote. "I also have a name, it's Jocelyn Benson. And we sent applications, not ballots. Just like my GOP colleagues in Iowa, Georgia, Nebraska and West Virginia."

Jocelyn Benson ✓
@JocelynBenson

Hi! 🤚 I also have a name, it's Jocelyn Benson. And we sent applications, not ballots. Just like my GOP colleagues in Iowa, Georgia, Nebraska and West Virginia.

> 🔵 Donald J. Trump ✓ @realDonaldTr... ·10h
> Breaking: Michigan sends absentee ballots to 7.7 million people ahead of Primaries and the General Election. This was done illegally and without authorization by a rogue Secretary of State. I will ask to hold up funding to Michig...
> Show this thread

I knew he would punch back. Which he did, again calling me a "rogue Secretary of State" and again threatening to withhold federal funding for the entire state if I didn't change plans.

So I responded. Again. Trembling as I typed.

"Hi again," I wrote. "Still wrong. Every Michigan registered voter has a right to vote by mail. I have the authority & responsibility to make sure that they know how to exercise this right—just like my GOP colleagues are doing in GA, IA, NE and WV. Also, again, my name is Jocelyn Benson."

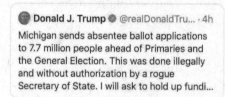

Jocelyn Benson ✔
@JocelynBenson

Hi again. Still wrong. Every Michigan registered voter has a right to vote by mail. I have the authority & responsibility to make sure that they know how to exercise this right - just like my GOP colleagues are doing in GA, IA, NE and WV. Also, again, my name is Jocelyn Benson.

🔵 Donald J. Trump ✔ @realDonaldTru... · 4h
Michigan sends absentee ballot applications to 7.7 million people ahead of Primaries and the General Election. This was done illegally and without authorization by a rogue Secretary of State. I will ask to hold up fundi...

I was, a lowly, unknown state election official trying to do my job the best I could during a global pandemic. My goal was simple: to ensure that our elections were safe and secure, and that every voter knew how to participate in them. That's it. Never in a million years did I expect a sitting president to attack me, spread lies about my work, and ridicule me on social media.

And yet, here we were.

When powerful people attack you, even if they are the most powerful person in the free world, you can still rise up and confidently respond with truth and strength. In that moment, I was grounded in a purpose and determined to hold someone with far more power than me accountable for his lies, disrespect, and bullying behavior.

Whether it's 1965, 2020, or 2065, we must stand up to people abusing their positions of authority. Even, perhaps especially, when it's scary, we must do so with purpose, intention, honesty, and maybe a little humor.

The back-and-forth between me and President Trump back in May 2020 immediately thrust me into the national spotlight. Under that pressure his attack was as strategic as my response was truthful: Trump was setting himself up to accuse me of rigging Michigan's elections if he were to lose. His decision to attack a little-known state official was the first indication that he was laying the groundwork for a larger scheme, I explained.

That point was picked up by national media, many of who framed the exchange as a president trying to intimidate a state election official. For me, it was a chance to show the nation how we in Michigan respond to bullies: Don't blink.

"Michigan's secretary of state called him out," historian Heather Cox Richardson noted.[3] "Insisting on the reality that belies his narrative, she repeat[ed]: 'My name is Jocelyn Benson.' . . . [I]nvoking someone's name makes them a power to be reckoned with," she said. "In this case, a woman doing her job, insisting on reality that interrupts Trump's narrative, repeatedly demands that he use her name. . . . At a time when senators and government officials appear to have ceded their power to Trump, it is ordinary Americans like Jocelyn Benson, ordinary women like Jocelyn Benson, who are standing up to him. 'Hi!' she wrote. 'I also have a name.' . . . That's exactly what the president is afraid of."

I had a name and a purpose: to speak the truth and stand up to a bully who was lying. In doing so I found the power of being a purposeful warrior. It is sometimes the only way we can seek justice for someone intent on abusing their authority to harm, deride, and dehumanize us.

Standing Up to Bullies Together

I was the first election official President Trump attacked that year. But I was far from the last. In the months that followed he continually took aim at me and other election officials with false, often cruel, accusations.

As the attacks escalated, it became clear we'd need a coordinated team of "rogue" election officials from both sides of the aisle to consistently push back with the truth. We formed a group of statewide and local election administrators from Michigan, Pennsylvania, Wisconsin, Arizona, Nevada, and Georgia. We called ourselves Team Democracy. And in the lead-up to the November 2020 election we collectively emboldened each other to stand up to Trump, framing his unfair attacks and cowardly nicknames as tools he and his team deployed to create and reinforce a false narrative of election malfeasance.

It was clear to us that Trump's goal was to create a feeling of chaos, confusion, and fear, to divide, deceive, and deter voters from participating in the election and trusting the results. It was also apparent to us that we needed to react in a way that would send a message: His approach was unpatriotic and dangerous, whether from Trump or from any other leader.

So we focused on crafting responses to his varying accusations that would convey clarity, certainty, and the truth. We sought to redirect every deceptive arrow thrown our way toward a promise for American citizens that no matter where they voted or whom they voted for, their vote would count and they could trust the results of the elections to be an accurate reflection of the will of the people.

We approached November of that election year knowing that secretaries of state in these states would be on the front lines of battling an unprecedented, nationally coordinated effort to challenge, and potentially undo, the accurate results of a presidential election.

And we knew if those efforts were successful, democracy as we knew it would unravel. We would not allow the United States to become a country where powerful people could simply nullify election results they didn't like through intimidation and threats. So we found great purpose as warriors defending democracy, defying powerful politicians who lied about our integrity to further their own political agenda, knowing that the actions we took then would reverberate for decades to come.

Throughout 2020 we defied hateful rhetoric and violent threats from political figures with more power than us as we worked to protect legitimate and accurate election results. We fought for ourselves, our integrity, our oaths of office, the American voters, and our democracy. We embraced our duty to tell the truth and protect the will of the people—even if that meant going toe to toe with some of the most powerful people in America.

Because no matter how powerful they were or how powerless we felt, we were warriors with a purpose: to hold bullies—who traded in lies, division, and corruption—accountable.

Ultimately, in Michigan and nationwide, democracy prevailed in

2020. Standing together in our state and across the country, election officials were able to modernize voter registration systems to ensure that every eligible citizen could register and vote, in some cases even on Election Day itself. We educated all citizens about their right to vote from home and installed secure ballot drop boxes to give voters a safe and reliable option to return their ballot on time. We partnered with dozens of nonpartisan organizations, from the American Bar Association to major professional sports teams, to cut through the noise and give every voter the confidence and clarity they needed to exercise their right to vote. We worked overtime, with the truth on our side, to push back on the lies of a president who tried to confuse and obfuscate the voting process. We worked around the clock with voter advocates across the country to amplify the truth—not just about how to vote safely, securely, and with confidence, but also to shine a light on the deceptive tactics of politicians and to call out the real agenda behind them: to deter voter turnout.

We election officials activated our power as purposeful warriors to stand up, speak the truth, hold the powerful accountable, and help all voters to do the same.

And when the polls closed on election night in November 2020, we felt we had prevailed in that fight. Not because any candidate had won or lost. But because every state in the country had administered a smooth, seamless, secure election, in which more citizens voted—on both sides of the aisle—than ever before. The deceptive tactics to deter voters had not succeeded in discouraging citizens from casting their ballots.

But this was all far from over.

When Bullies Punch Back

In Michigan and around the country in November 2020, after the polls closed and every valid vote was counted, the unofficial results were announced. Trump and his most ardent supporters were not happy they had lost the election.

So they entered the next phase of their plan, falsely claiming they had won, spreading misinformation about the security of our elections, and hatching a plan to get Congress to override the results.

In the seventy-eight days between when the polls closed on November 3, 2020, and the presidential inauguration on January 20, 2021, citizens nationwide were inundated with a storm of lies. The "big lie," as it became known, the false notion that Trump had won the election, was spread through meritless lawsuits, sham legislative hearings, bizarre press conferences, and protests fueled by falsehoods. People unhappy with the election results—many of whom sincerely believed Trump had won, others who knew he hadn't but lied about it anyway—tried to interfere with the counting of valid votes, block the certification of accurate election results, threaten election officials, and attempt to submit multiple false, alternate slates of electors to the National Archives from Michigan, Wisconsin, Nevada, Arizona, Pennsylvania, and New Mexico.

We saw all of this escalate to the tragedy at the United States Capitol on January 6, when thousands stormed the building in a violent, deadly effort to block the counting of the electoral votes.

As an election administrator I always welcome questions about the elections process, even challenges to the results and audits to affirm their integrity. But legitimate accusations require evidence of wrongdoing. And these challengers had none.

In fact, at no point, ever, in all the challenges to the 2020 election results, did anyone produce a shred of evidence that those results were inaccurate.

Prior to Election Day 2020 we could never have anticipated the lengths to which a losing presidential candidate and their most ardent supporters would go to lie to the public about, interfere with, and seek to overturn the results of a fair election. We'd never faced that level of pushback and suspicion before, especially absent any evidence of wrongdoing or fraud.

Election professionals always hope for the best while planning for every possible contingency. And in 2020, we did anticipate that there would be some attempt to claim victory—prematurely and potentially falsely—before the unofficial results had been fully tallied.

So shortly after the polls closed in Michigan on election night, my colleagues and I held a press conference where we made clear that regardless of which presidential candidate emerged victorious, we all had a responsibility and duty to "ensure truth—and democracy—prevail in the days ahead. . . .

"We are going to count every single vote in the state of Michigan," I said to state and national media. "No matter how long it takes, no matter what candidates say, we are going to work methodically and meticulously to count every single valid ballot, and that—and only that—will determine who wins every race on the ballot in the state of Michigan.[4]

"It is critical," I said, "that we work to protect our democracy and the voice of our voters by ensuring every valid ballot is counted, that we do not give space to anyone who attempts to make premature declarations about the outcome of any races in Michigan. And I am relying on the media and voters alike, in partnership with my office and out of respect for the will of the voters and the work of the volunteers tabulating these ballots, to stand vigilant with us."

As soon as legally permissible, we began sharing election results with local and national media. By 4:30 p.m., nearly every jurisdiction in the state had reported its unofficial results and media outlets began declaring Joe Biden the winner of Michigan's sixteen electoral votes.

We expected at that point that the protests, threats, and attacks would diminish.

They escalated.

A crowd soon grew outside a convention center in Detroit. Inside the center, election observers from both political parties calmly witnessed poll workers tabulate the final remaining ballots in the state. But outside, the crowd, many of whom were armed and open-carrying pistols, became unhinged. They broke windows, demanding entry into the area where ballots were being securely tallied. They yelled and screamed at the poll workers to stop the counting. Without evidence, they made accusations of fraud and wrongdoing.

These disruptions continued for days and were soon accompanied by a growing number of meritless lawsuits—sixty-four in Michigan alone—seeking to intervene with the certification of the official results. The challenges escalated on November 17, 2020, at the local meeting of the Wayne County Board of Canvassers, where two Democrats and two Republicans gathered to certify Detroit's election results. That same evening, Michigan's top legislative leaders traveled to a meeting at the White House with Trump and Rudy Giuliani, now acting as his attorney, and discussed potential ways to intervene with the certification of the final election results.

Throughout it all, the purposeful warrior ethos of election officials in battleground states held strong. In Michigan we established a website portal for citizens to submit questions about rumors they might hear so that they could receive fact-based, trustworthy information in response. We also worked with our partners in neighboring states to help counter the growing number of falsehoods nationwide, knowing that only by locking arms and amplifying the truth could we emerge out of this contentious moment with the election results intact.

On November 23, 2020, the Board of State Canvassers met to finalize and certify the final election results. The board, comprised of two Democrats and two Republicans appointed by their respective state party chairs, had a very clear legal and ministerial duty to certify the election. Yet the GOP, as *Politico* reported later, directed the Republican appointees to reject to the certification and "drag things out, to further muddy the election waters and delegitimize the process."[5] This would have forced the courts to either certify the election or, possibly, empower the Republican-led state legislature to reject the results as invalid and instead direct the state's electoral votes to the candidate of their choosing.

In reflection of this plan the Trump campaign even recruited a second, "alternate" slate of Trump electors, each of whom signed false elector certificates that were submitted to the United States National Archives to erroneously award Michigan's electoral votes to Trump over Biden.

It was a detailed, coordinated effort rooted in lies and in violation of the law and the Constitution.

Michigan was in a particular spotlight that year because our results were set to be finalized first among six targeted battleground states.

That made it even more important for the nation that the plan to challenge the certification of election results was stymied in our state. And defying the demands of his party, one of the two Republican appointees to the Board of Canvassers went rogue, told the truth, and voted to certify the results.

"We have a clear legal duty to certify the results of the election," Aaron Van Langevelde explained in casting his decisive vote for certification that day. "We cannot and should not go beyond that."

In speaking the truth—and voting to certify—Aaron Van Langevelde gave the country clarity and confidence that the will of the people in Michigan would rule the day. One hour after his vote and statement, we saw a glimmer of a light at the end of the post-election tunnel as Trump's team began to take steps toward what appeared to be the transition of power to then President-elect Biden. President Trump even seemed to accept and endorse a peaceful transition of power, saying that beginning the transition was "in the best interest of our Country."[6]

And yet.

In the five other battleground states that had yet to finalize, or certify, their results—Wisconsin, Pennsylvania, Georgia, Arizona, and Nevada—Trump and an array of his advisers continued to pressure every official they could reach to stop the legal certification of each state's election results. And amazingly, even after the results in Michigan had been certified, their efforts in our state to block the delivery of the state's official electoral college votes to Congress renewed and intensified. In early December, Rudy Giuliani came to Michigan to allege various false accusations of election fraud in a state legislative hearing so atrociously nonsensical and fallacious it was parodied on *Saturday Night Live*. Two days later protesters gathered outside my home, shouting at me to "stop the steal" of a now-certified election where the will of the voters was clear, verifiable, and unequivocal.

In Georgia, even more egregious attempts to threaten and pressure election officials unfolded in a series of phone calls from the White House to Republican officials, culminating in an unprecedented call and demand from Trump to Secretary of State Brad Raffensperger on January 2, 2021. During the conversation Trump, along with lawyers from his team, including Cleta Mitchell, John Eastman, and Rudy Giuliani, falsely claimed Trump had won the majority of votes in Georgia.[7]

"We won very substantially in Georgia," Trump said in a recording of the call that was later released to the public. "You even see it by rally size." Citing numerous conspiracy theories, from ballot stuffing to dead people voting, Trump and his team asked Raffensperger to "recalculate" the results in his favor.

"Well, President Trump," the secretary said in response, "we don't agree that you have won." He went on to explain: "The challenge that you have is, the data you have is wrong. The numbers are the numbers, the numbers don't lie."

"So look," Trump said, after nearly an hour of recounting previously disproven allegations and presenting no evidence to back up his claims, "all I want to do is this. I just want to find 11,780 votes, which is one more than we have because we won the state."

Raffensperger refused.

"You know, that's a criminal offense," Trump suggested. "That's a big risk to you."

The next day Trump attacked Secretary Raffensperger on social media, falsely claiming he "was unwilling, or unable, to answer questions such as the 'ballots under table' scam, ballot destruction, out of state 'voters', dead voters, and more. He has no clue!"[8]

Standing up for himself and his colleagues, for truth and democracy,

Raffensperger responded. "Respectfully, President Trump," he punched back, "what you're saying is not true. The truth will come out."[9]

Team Democracy in Georgia went to work. Raffensperger's team released a recording of the call to *The Washington Post* and *The New York Times*. In doing so, they stood up for themselves and all the professional election officials in Georgia enduring Trump's continued public lies about their work and integrity. With truth on their side—and evidence to back it up—they exposed a president's lies, holding him accountable in defense of themselves, their state, and their country.

Raffensperger was met with praise nationwide, lauded as a hero and a man of integrity. But far noisier were the attacks he received from his own party members who withdrew their support. The chair of the Georgia Republican Party accused Raffensperger, a fellow Republican, of "lawlessness," and the state party voted to censure the secretary for "dereliction of his constitutional duty" over the presidential election. Trump and the two sitting US senators from Georgia—David Perdue and Kelly Loeffler—consistently trashed Raffensperger for asserting that Georgia ran a fair election and later endorsed a primary opponent to run against him.

All of this collectively demonstrated to us the lesson that even when you stand up to bullies, even when truth and the law are on your side, even when the stakes of a historic presidential election hang in the balance, bullies will punch back.

For Raffensperger, the death threats targeted his wife, Tricia, who received several horrific text messages—some anonymous, others from "raffensperger@revenge.us."[10]

"You and your family will be killed very slowly," read one text sent late at night to her personal cell phone. That followed two others sent anonymously—one warning that a family member was "going to have a very unfortunate incident" and another that said "We plan for the death of you and your family every day."

The chilling threats escalated to such an extent that Brad and Tricia Raffensperger asked their children and grandchildren to not visit them for several months. "I couldn't have them come to my house anymore," Tricia later told Reuters. "You don't know if these people are actually going to act on this stuff."[11]

Laudably, in the face of these harrowing challenges, the attacks, the threats, the isolation, and the very real danger to himself and his family, Raffensperger never wavered from his duty to stand up for himself, the voters of his state, and democracy. "If the good walk off the field and leave the field to the bad, then the bad wins," he said.[12] He continued to push back on Trump's bullying and lies—testifying before the congressional January 6 committee, spending hours with federal investigators, and cooperating with a criminal probe in Fulton County, Georgia, that resulted in sixteen indictments against Trump and several of his co-conspirators.

Raffensperger was not the only recipient of the president's ire and lies. His experience became a high-profile illustration of the challenges several election officials throughout the country endured in the aftermath of the 2020 election. But Trump didn't only attack state-level election officials in the months following his loss. No, he punched down even further.

One of the most consequential attacks came when Trump and his team took aim at local election officials in Fulton County. It started with a video of election workers taken at State Farm Arena in Atlanta. In it, Trump's team alleged, was evidence of flagrant ballot stuffing, fraud, and drug use. Raffensperger responded with the accurate assertion that Rudy Giuliani had selectively edited the video to further a falsehood.

The election officials at the heart of that false allegation were Ruby Freeman and Wandrea "Shaye" Moss. Trump and Giuliani claimed that video footage showed them tampering with the vote count by passing a USB drive—in reality, it was a ginger mint. After a conservative PAC posted the video and amplified Trump and Giuliani's accusations, both women received a torrent of hateful threats with racist undertones. Trump supporters showed up to the home of one of their family members, bursting through the doors demanding to make a "citizen's arrest." Before long Freeman and Moss were afraid to say their own names in public for fear of being attacked.

"For my entire professional life, I was Lady Ruby," Freeman told the congressional January 6 committee in sworn testimony. "Now, I won't even introduce myself by my name anymore. . . . I'm worried about who is listening. I've lost my name, and I've lost my reputation. I've lost my sense of security, all because a group of people, starting with number 45 and his ally Rudy Giuliani, decided to scapegoat me and my daughter, Shaye, to push their own lies about how the presidential election was stolen . . . ."[13]

"There is nowhere I feel safe," Freeman said. "Nowhere. Do you know how it feels to have the president of the United States target you? The president of the United States is supposed to represent every American. Not to target one. But he targeted me, Lady Ruby, a small business owner, a mother, a proud American citizen, who stood up to help Fulton County run an election in the middle of the pandemic."[14]

Like Miss Ruby and her daughter Shaye, many other local election workers in battleground states faced lies and attacks from a sitting American president and his lawyers and supporters. Tina Barton, a local clerk in Rochester, Michigan, received a voicemail filled with explicit language threatening her family. Detroit City Clerk Janice Winfrey was sent photos of a dead body with a message to imagine that body as her daughter. Elsewhere in Michigan, Antrim County Clerk Sheryl Guy had to go into hiding after a harmless error was used to falsely fuel a national conspiracy theory. Al Schmidt, a former Republican city commissioner in Philadelphia who oversaw that city's vote counting in 2020, received threats that named his children and included his address and photos of his house. Bill Gates, a Republican member of the Maricopa County Board of Supervisors in Arizona, was told that he and his family would be slaughtered.

These heartbreaking stories underscore the impact of the lies and threats that dominated the lives of election officials in battleground states in 2020. We signed up to make sure that elections went smoothly and securely, and that every eligible citizen could vote. Yet we found ourselves tasked with another purpose as well: standing up to powerful bullies, from local party officials to lawyers to state and federal legislators to the president of the United States, all of whom spread lies about our work and made threats to our safety and our lives to further their own political agenda. These lies and threats came from the highest level and targeted Republican, Democratic, and independent officials alike, many working in small towns and cities and rural counties throughout the country—regular people, our neighbors and community members, civil servants who go back and forth to their offices and homes, dropping off or picking up children and groceries along the way. As we went about the daily activities that so many of us take for granted, we were threatened for simply doing our jobs.

We experienced firsthand that when you stand up to bullies they tend to punch back—sometimes in the form of even worse abuse than you initially endured.

But that doesn't mean it's OK to cave to them, or not to stand up in the first place.

Standing up to bullies is not easy.

But it's necessary.

As election officials in 2020, many of us women, we all saw the importance of responding to the lies and threats of those more powerful than us. Doing so required us to be warriors with a purpose—defending the legal, valid votes of every American citizen, and the accurate election outcomes that resulted. As purposeful warriors, we could not and would not allow fear to prevent us from protecting our elections and defending every voice and every vote. Because we knew the threats against us were also threats to democracy and to the millions of Americans who have a right to choose our leaders and hold them accountable.

I stood up to Donald Trump when he lied about me. Just as any one of us should be prepared to do with any president, or any leader, who uses their authority to belittle others with lies and threats.

Pushing back on his lies was grueling, exhausting, demoralizing, and discouraging.

Yet in refusing to allow the lies to stand, I found that my small voice could match his power.

How to Go Rogue and Stand Up to Bullies in Your Life

The story of the 2020 election and its aftermath underscores the dangers of politicians who, without any evidence, attempt to delegitimize legitimate election outcomes. And it also highlights that the power of the people, armed with truth, will always be greater than that of the people in power who bully with lies. The election officials who stood up to a president that year were ordinary people. We were not looking for the spotlight and we did not want to be seen as heroes.

And we also had a clear-eyed view of the harm that would come if we allowed bullies to get away with undermining our work, our elections, and the voice and votes of the American people.

So we took steps that anyone can take to stand up to the bullies on your own doorstep. We countered the lies with facts. That meant exposing efforts to deceive voters about our elections and voting processes and calling them out for their true goal: discouraging people from believing in democracy and the power of the voter.

We refused to back down, even when we were threatened or ridiculed. This meant standing my ground even when people were literally on my front lawn, demanding I come out so that they could confront me about the results of the election. It also meant that, even though I wanted to crawl back under my covers the morning President Trump attacked me on social media, I had to stand up and push back—with truth. And a little bit of humor.

And we didn't go into battle alone. It's a tactic of bullies to isolate and separate as a way of gaining or maintaining power. Building your own "tribe" of support is something I'll talk about later in the book, but whether you find strength in numbers or power in connecting to a broader community of people who have faced similar abuse and challenges, it's critical to realize you're not alone in your quest to hold the bad guys accountable.

As we endured the inevitable backlash to standing up to Trump, the collective strength of our bipartisan community of professional election officials helped us carry the day and emerge on the other side of the election emboldened with a stronger determination to do our jobs well and protect every vote, every voice, and every election's results.

In his 1986 Nobel Peace Prize lecture, Elie Wiesel warned that "there may be times when we are powerless to prevent injustice, but there must never be a time when we fail to protest." Standing up to bullies who seek to abuse their authority, ridicule with lies, or divide with deception will always be necessary. Doing so requires us all to be warriors, purposefully coming together to stand up for ourselves, each other, the truth, and our world.

Chapter 3

If I Stay Silent

What chance do we have?
The question is, "What choice?"

JYN ERSO[1]

Being a purposeful warrior means fighting to advance an innovative idea, promote a bold vision, and work to build something new. It requires that we stand up to the "bad guys," as my son would say, and refuse to stay silent or on the sidelines in the face of a wrong, or injustice, as Viola Liuzzo's story demonstrates. It also involves knowing the consequences of staying silent.

Speaking out for or working to further something you believe in requires you to shine a light on something that others might not see or notice. This involves risks—you might rock a boat, upset an applecart, or offer advice that might fall on deaf or uninterested ears. There will be a lot of proverbial wind in your face. So you'll need a strategy to stay the course, reach people, and move the needle, rooted in a clear understanding of why the cost of staying silent is much greater than any risk in speaking out.

There's a story about Robert F. Kennedy's 1968 presidential campaign that's stuck with me since I first read about it in Thurston Clarke's book *The Last Campaign*.[2]

RFK was in Omaha in May 1968, the night before Nebraska's presidential primary, speaking to "four thousand largely white, middle-class students" at Creighton University. He "delivered a gentle speech," Clarke writes, "encouraging the students to view their education as a tool for bettering the lives of the poor."[3]

Then he began taking questions. It started with a question about his opponent Eugene McCarthy, and quickly turned to a discussion about students, like those present, who were deferring service in Vietnam under a policy that allowed full-time students to avoid the draft indefinitely. Kennedy denounced the policy, arguing that it was unfair and that student deferments should be replaced with a lottery so that everyone, including the students in the room, could be called to serve in Vietnam.

The students booed.

According to Clarke their negative reaction did not deter Kennedy. He'd anticipated it ahead of time, in fact, and he seemed to embrace it and use it to fuel his response. Noting that the room was full of white college students, he implored them, "Look around you. How many black faces do you see here? How many American Indians? How many Mexican-Americans? The fact is, if you look at any regiment or division of paratroopers in Vietnam, forty-five percent of them are black. How can you accept this?"[4]

Kennedy held up a mirror to the room—a room he needed to win over to win the Nebraska primary the following day. He didn't tell the audience what they wanted to hear. He told them the truth, denouncing a poorly developed military draft policy that exempted college students and subsequently led far too many Americans of color to be sent to the front lines of the Vietnam War while privileged white men stayed at home.

For Kennedy, speaking out against a policy that was unjust before an audience that was directly benefiting from that inequality was the right thing to do. But he needed to do it in a way that wouldn't cost him the electoral victory he was in town to campaign for.

"How can you accept this?" Kennedy pushed the crowd, according to Clarke. "You're the most exclusive minority in the world. Are you going to sit on your duffs and do nothing?"[5]

"There is a great moral force in the United States," he went on, "about the wrongs of the Federal Government and all the mistakes Lyndon Johnson has made, and how Congress has failed to pass legislation dealing with civil rights. And yet, when it comes down to yourselves and your own individual lives, then you say students should be draft-deferred."[6]

When he finished, he had shamed the Creighton students into "a red-faced silence."[7]

There Kennedy was, refusing to stay silent, the night before an election in which these students and other Nebraska voters would be casting a ballot for or against him in a contested presidential primary. Kennedy didn't waver, nor did he allow the whims of his audience to define his position. He didn't do what many politicians courting votes would have done in this circumstance—smile, nod, listen silently, and perhaps even convey a complicit agreement.

Instead of equivocate, pivot, or dodge, Kennedy demanded justice, equality, and fairness because he believed that the issue of student deferments "contravened a concept central to his patriotism: equality of sacrifice."[8]

"What he did was really not all that mystical," the former Kennedy staffer John Nolan later recalled to Clarke. "All it requires is someone who knows himself and has some courage."[9]

Speaking up on behalf of yourself or others is usually not the easy path. It's uncomfortable and scary. It leads to criticism, personal threats, and attacks, made more difficult when we know saying nothing and staying silent would have kept us safe.

Kennedy knew this. He lived it.

But he also knew the inherent value in speaking the truth anyway— and not allowing anyone else to define who he was. He had his own ideas about the right thing to do and what he wanted to contribute to the world. Kennedy raised his voice with moral clarity because he had seen firsthand that if he didn't, he'd be complicit in enabling corruption and inequality.

Kennedy ultimately won the Nebraska primary the day after his speech by a large margin. He had gone into the rally with Creighton University students intending to speak out for the thousands of poor Americans who were disproportionally bearing the brunt of the Vietnam War, as he had done on other college campuses. He was prepared to withstand the inevitable criticism for speaking up about the draft.

But in challenging the college students, he succeeded in doing something more. Though his campaign for president ended in horrific tragedy, Clarke writes that he "convinced millions of Americans that he was a good man, perhaps a great man."[10]

Kennedy's warrior campaign for president is still iconic today because it demonstrated to a nation what authentic service—and bold, courageous leadership—could look like. He showed the people he was campaigning to lead that in raising his voice and speaking the truth, he'd seek to "educate rather than manipulate them, reconcile rather than divide them, engage them in a dialogue rather than feed them the message of the day, appeal to their better angels instead of their wallets, and demand sacrifice instead of promising comfort."[11]

This, perhaps, was his greatest victory. His last campaign showed public servants of all backgrounds, in every industry, that it's not only possible to be a good person, "perhaps a great one," to speak the truth and lead with integrity. It's the right thing to do.

As warriors we refuse to stay silent. We speak the truth to define, or redefine, what's right, appropriate, or fair. And in raising our voices and championing our cause we not only articulate what we stand for or what we're fighting against, we also avoid the consequences of in-action.

Raise Your Voice, and Have a Plan

As Michigan's chief election officer for nearly a decade, I proudly bore the costs of raising my voice to defend democracy and speak truth to power. It wasn't easy, but I knew if I didn't embrace those costs I'd be opening the door for others to cloud the reality of our election integrity. I was unwilling to cede my voice to anyone who wouldn't tell the accurate story about the security of our elections, so I grabbed the mic and started talking. Yes, I was met with vitriol and threats. But the risks of staying silent were greater. I needed to tell the true story of how hard we were working to ensure that all valid votes—and only valid votes—were counted, and that the results of the election were an accurate reflection of the will of the people.

Years before that election, when I was the dean of Wayne State Law School, I'd had similar experiences that underscored the importance of raising my voice and the risk of staying silent. I learned that it's not just about speaking out, but also having a plan for what comes next.

I started teaching law as a professor at a very young age—twenty-seven. Eight years later, I was asked to lead the school, an appointment that made me the youngest woman in the history of the United States to serve as the dean of an accredited law school.

There's a bit more to that story. A couple of years before I became dean, things had declined significantly at the school—similar to the downturn that the city where Wayne State is located, Detroit, was enduring at the same time. Incoming student applications were down, the job market made it challenging for graduates to land well-paying positions, and our *U.S. News & World Report* ranking had plummeted into the bottom tier of all schools nationwide.

As a young law professor approaching my mid-thirties, I had some concerns. I also had some ideas on how I could turn things around. So I stepped up, spoke out, and applied to serve as interim dean to help right the ship.

I'm not sure if the university president thought it'd be a headline-grabbing novelty to select a woman in her mid-thirties to lead the law school or whether he seriously thought I could do the job. Either way, the number of people wanting to step in and lead the law school out of the abyss was minimal, and so they gave me the gig.

Many in our university community celebrated the news. Here was a young, fresh face coming in to lead a law school that had recently fallen on hard times and needed new leadership.

Others were more than a little skeptical that I had what it would take to fix things. I was young and untested. Aside from a statewide political campaign a few years earlier, I'd never really "run" anything before. And now, they complained, we're giving her the reins?

Nevertheless, I took office raring to go. I had lofty ideals and an ambitious strategic plan to take the school from the bottom rank of law schools nationwide to the top fifty. I was not shy in speaking out about all the things that would have to change to move us forward. Budgetary decisions would need to be revisited, alumni reengaged, and departmental structures reorganized; faculty would need to start publishing more. We'd all have to do our part, I explained in my first address to the school upon taking office, to revive our school and reclaim our place in the national rankings.

I created a ten-year timeline and presented it to my colleagues.

A few of them laughed. Others just stared at me with no reaction at all.

And then they all voted to reject it.

There I was, a purposeful warrior who was on a mission to rework, revamp, and renovate the struggling school. Taking the job and raising my voice, I sought to clearly identify and lay out exactly what we all needed to do next. I'd thought that would begin to move things forward.

But it was merely the first step.

Yes, I needed to use my voice to call out unsaid truths and communicate a vision for dramatic reforms—even if it invited jeers or derision.

It wouldn't be enough, however, to only present or propose the path forward. I also needed to develop and execute a plan and build a team to get there.

And that, I soon realized, would be more difficult than I'd thought.

For example, as a young woman, I found not long after assuming the role of dean that many colleagues who had treated me fairly for years now approached me with skepticism in my new role as their boss. To be fair, many of them had been teaching or running parts of the law school for decades, some starting their careers there long before I'd been born. Who was I to come in and tell them to change everything they were doing or redefine their job description?

I took the time to listen, learn, and see things from their perspective. Through many coffees, lunches, and phone calls I helped open some up to embracing expanded roles, new curricula, or added responsibilities. Some insisted on financial incentives or new titles, and more than a few decided to leave the school entirely rather than step up their game to enable us all to achieve more.

I also dealt with the fact that many of my colleagues, fellow law professors who had their own ideas and visions for the school, believed that my proposals were not "well-thought-out or realistic," as one said. "Too ambitious," others remarked. How would we find funds to offer greater scholarship support, reengage our alumni to mentor and invest in our current students, and grow our budget in order to recruit more talented and academically successful applicants and faculty? It wasn't long before some even began looking for someone else to take my place as dean—without even giving me a chance to prove their expectations wrong.

That was gutting. Less than three months on the job and I was already being defined as a likely failure because of what others perceived as my inexperience, youth, and lofty goals.

Still, I didn't waver. I stayed focused on my goals, plans, and purpose. And I went to work. I spoke out in support of my vision for getting the school into the top-fifty law schools in the country. Delivering the law school's first-ever, now annual "State of the Law School" address, I declared that "jobs, jobs, jobs" would be our new mantra for current students and built a vision for training our students for the jobs of the future. I laid out my ambitious plan for the law school's success and described how I'd developed it with data, innovative funding models, and best practices to replicate from top-tier law schools. I defined new ways to generate revenue and aggressive and relentless strategies for convincing billionaire alumni like the Miami Dolphins owner Stephen Ross and the Cleveland Cavaliers owner Dan Gilbert to invest in and support their alma mater.

Then I asked everyone, the entire law school and extended university community, to hold me accountable. Transparency was our friend, I told them, committing to posting my timeline, my strategy, and the metrics I'd use to evaluate myself and our team on our website for all to see.

I set out purposefully to redefine what was possible for the school—and then followed it up with a plan and a strategy to implement it. It not only helped me overcome the pushback from folks resistant to change; it also ensured I made good on my vision and was able to get it done.

Our ultimate goal, I said to all, was to move the law school out of the bottom ranking of law schools into the top fifty. Getting there began with improving our ability to recruit talented students from top colleges across the country and offer them competitive scholarships. To fund those scholarships, I worked to engage our massive and successful alumni network—most lawyers in Michigan graduated from Wayne Law, after all—and asked them not only to donate to us but also to commit to mentoring our students and helping them find well-paying jobs in an increasingly competitive employment market. We also worked to increase the racial and gender diversity of our faculty and student body, recognizing that doing so would both create a more inclusive, safe, and welcoming community and increase the variety of perspectives in our classrooms' learning environment. I also set clear goals and metrics for myself and for others to meet on a weekly, monthly, and yearly basis—and acted collaboratively and transparently to develop and implement a plan that moved all the numbers in the right direction.

And I worked hard, really hard, to push our plan forward. I drove myself across the state, sometimes through whiteout blizzards or torrential rainstorms, to visit every undergraduate campus in Michigan and speak to future law students about the virtues of attending law school at Wayne State, in a historical moment of rebirth for the long-struggling city of Detroit. We reduced the overall cost of tuition for all law students through expanded scholarship offerings, recruited more alumni to give back to the school and mentor current students, and placed more graduates in high-paying jobs upon graduation.

Combining hard work, passion, persistence, vision, and clear goals is the essence of how a purposeful warrior moves forward. We not only speak out and raise our voices, we follow up by aggressively chasing the metrics for our success, and we fight hard to meet our goals.

For a law dean it was a winning strategy. In my first year of my deanship, and every year that followed, Wayne State Law School went up in the national rankings—surpassing other law schools throughout the country and moving up dozens of spots in the top one hundred, quickly rising to be the second-highest-ranked law school in the state. Sure enough, ten years later it rose to be ranked 55 out of nearly 200 law schools listed in the *U.S. News & World Report*'s 2025 Best Law School rankings.[12]

It all began with raising my voice and offering to define a better future for the school. I told our story, laid out a vision for a better future, and then employed data, anecdotes, and facts to demonstrate our success. I was determined not to allow anyone else to place limits on our possibilities. I continued to speak out, sharing and amplifying facts, building a reputation and brand for the school that exhibited our strengths and sharing them with our alumni, prospective students, and the public.

I found every step of the way that when you refuse to stay silent, you don't just shed a light on wrongs or injustices. You also redefine what is possible—for yourself and for others. Standing for what was right as the dean meant talking about what we could achieve, developing a plan, and refusing to allow others' lack of faith to compel me into silence or inaction.

Wayne Law is now one of the nation's top law schools. Stepping up, raising my voice, and following up with a plan took us there. My voice broke through and brought others along, and together we found success.

That doesn't always happen.

When You Raise Your Voice and People Don't Listen

Soon after my appointment as dean, I began meeting monthly with the university official who set our budget. A big part of my plan entailed better utilizing our existing financial resources—and also identifying new sources of revenue to help us meet our aggressive goals.

Under a long-standing agreement with the university and every school within it, all the tuition and revenue we brought in went directly to the university's general fund. After that, every school within the university, including the law school, had its entire subsequent budget and revenue allowance allocated and determined through a process that one person—the university's budget director—managed and oversaw. He answered only to the provost, who gave him almost unilateral authority in determining how much money each school would receive for its budget each year.

The budget director met monthly with every dean to review the respective schools' goals and operations. He was an overseer charged with evaluating our expenditures, reviewing plans for additional revenue generation, and tracking all expenses. Because he managed and ulti-mately determined each school's budget, it was critical that each dean maintained a good relationship with the director if we wanted to have the funds we needed to meet our goals.

.It was about a year into my term when the harassment began.

The budget director started requesting more frequent meetings with me—one-on-one. Every other dean met with him once a month, with their school's respective budget director. But me? I was told to meet with him every other week if I wanted my budget requests to re-ceive consideration.

I thought maybe it was just because I was young and new to the job. How nice he is, I told myself, offering extra time to help me shape a strategy to match the budget allocations with our school's needs.

After a few months I submitted a budget request for an increase in funding to cover necessary student expenses.

Meet me for a drink, was his response. We can discuss your request then.

OK, I thought. I've always preferred Diet Coke to alcohol, but sure, I guess meeting the budget director for drinks was what all the deans did to persuade the university to grant our budget requests. Like agree-ing to a round of golf or a game of pickleball, this was how to spend time building a trustful rapport with people making consequential decisions about our future. This is what I need to do to get things done, I assured myself.

Then, a few weeks later, he invited me to a baseball game—to dis-cuss the budget, of course.

I love baseball. I am a passionate fan of the game. I literally had my wedding rehearsal dinner at a baseball stadium. So yeah, I was not go-ing to turn down an invite to see the Detroit Tigers play.

And in retrospect, I'm sure he knew that. This invite seemed a little odd. So I asked my associate dean to join us, to avoid any presumption of impropriety. We went to the game, all three of us. My associate dean, who was male, sat in the middle.

No mixed signals here, I thought. Go Tigers.

But still, something was off. Throughout the game I felt awkward and uncomfortable, and I began to have a nagging feeling in my gut. Were all the deans expected to be this social with the budget director just to get our requests fulfilled?

Not long after the baseball game I started being more intentional about ensuring my staff accompanied me to any meeting with the budget director, thinking that would protect me and address my uneasiness with our interactions.

Then the incessant texts began.

While I was working at my desk, my phone would beep with a message from him, asking where I was and requesting spontaneous meetings. At one point he surreptitiously took photos of me walking through a hallway and sent them to me. "I'm watching you," he wrote in the accompanying text. It gave me chills. And made me nauseous.

It wasn't long before I started dreading coming to work, loathing interactions with him and resenting how I felt I had to continue playing along or face consequences in the form of deep budget cuts.

And I was mad at myself. Despite all I had done in my life to position myself as a fearless warrior, steadfast in my confident, assertive self, I was alarmingly ill-equipped and unprepared in that moment. I knew his behavior was wrong. I wanted to raise my voice and call him out.

But I was afraid. And that fear governed my actions, convincing me that I could endure his predatory behavior if it meant having my budget requests approved. My goal was to serve and grow the law school. I could handle this awkwardness to get there.

I found myself buried under a debilitating worry about speaking the truth to anyone, be it either confiding privately to a friend or colleague, or making some more public statement. How would people react? Would I be blamed? Did I do something to deserve this or bring it on myself? Had I collected enough proof of his inappropriate behavior to protect me from the inevitable denial and likely retaliation?

I struggled with this for almost an entire year. As a young female leader, I felt I had a responsibility to project strength, confidence, and a sense that I could handle anything. And here I was, unable to handle this situation.

I was supposed to be a problem solver. How could I not solve this?

But I had to try. I started out doing small things. One step at a time, I thought I could find my way through. I canceled meetings or asked others on my team to go in my place. I reached out to other deans to see if they'd experienced questionable behavior from the budget director. It helped a little, but it wasn't enough to undo the increasingly toxic environment.

Then one day I was working at my desk and got a phone call. In no uncertain terms, the budget director made clear in his call that if I spoke out about any of his inappropriate advances, which he considered demonstrations of his "stringent work ethic and extensive oversight," he would cut the law school budget. The cut, he warned, would be significant and, I realized, would make it impossible for me to fulfill my responsibilities and lofty goals as dean.

Such a clear threat should have energized me to speak out, right? Enough was enough.

Except that it wasn't. His call paralyzed me even further—which was, I'm sure, his intent. I was stuck. I didn't know where to go or what to do, or who to even trust to go to for advice.

I started hiding out in my office and declining to attend university events for fear of running into him.

Finally I got the nerve to get lunch with a few local female business leaders. I carefully described some of what I was experiencing, wondering if they'd ever dealt with similar behavior.

I was blown away. Every single woman I went to for advice said, essentially, "me too." Each one had her own similar stories of harassment, bullying, and other boorish behavior from superiors or colleagues in nearly every workplace.

Years later, the #MeToo movement would yield a reckoning for the far too many of us with similar—or much more tragic—stories. But in 2013 far too many of us were still silently suffering, trying to endure and carry on, succeeding in spite of harassment. It struck me how frequently we as women try to shoulder this burden on our own. And how, in a sisterhood of friends and colleagues, we shouldn't have to.

A few weeks later, my phone buzzed with another text message from the budget director. I still get a pit in my stomach remembering the moment I received it. "Hey there is a clothing optional 5K at the naked turtle lake resort just south of Battle creek Tomorrow," he wrote. "Who's in?"

Ugh, I thought, sickened by the brash audacity of the note. And with that, the final line was crossed. I'd hit my limit. That was it. There was no denying or explaining away this gross, awful, palpably inappropriate request.

Now the issue I had evaded for months had come to a head. It was time to speak out.

I saw clearly then that staying silent any longer in the face of this wildly unprofessional, practically predatory behavior would be complicit acceptance of his abuse of authority. Yes, speaking out meant stepping into an uncertain territory that would invite, among other things, retribution—from him and maybe others.

But by that point, I'd had enough. Were there others like me suffering in silence? If he would talk like this to a dean, how was he treating others in the university community?

I decided it was time to speak out and fight back.

My first step was to respond, in writing, stating unequivocally that his actions were inappropriate and made me very uncomfortable. This was "not an OK thing," I told him, for a university official to say to a dean.

Immediately the denials began.

"You're taking this out of context," he quickly retorted—as if there was some context in which asking a female dean of a law school to run in a naked road race with him was acceptable.

"Really?" I shot back. "Would you have sent this same text to [Engineering School Dean] Farhad?"

The next day he eliminated five hundred thousand dollars from my school's million-dollar budget.

Five hundred thousand dollars in scholarship funds. Gone. Why? Because I had spoken up. Because I had pushed back. Because I'd refused to stay silent.

It didn't matter. I was on the other side of my fear now, and I wasn't backing down.

I reached out to the provost and general counsel at the university and detailed the entire series of events. I came equipped with all the proof and receipts and examples I should have needed to make the case for them to take action. The harassment, the pestering, the requests for favors, the retaliation: all of it needed to stop.

Their reactions were not what I'd hoped.

"Boys will be boys," the provost said with a shrug, and moved on to her next meeting. Separately, the general counsel responded: "I think he just is one of those guys who still thinks it's the 1950s. Don't let his words bother you."

Oh, I get it, I thought petulantly. I'm supposed to just shake this off. Take it and accept it as appropriate behavior from a university official with power and authority over my budget. Got it.

They each promised me they would have a conversation with him.

Whether they did or not, I don't know. Either way, that was it. Nothing else happened. The budget director kept his job—and with it, all his authority over me, our school, and our finances. And I had to figure out how to deal with the big hole he'd blown in my budget.

I spoke out. But nothing immediately changed. Yes, in the years that followed, the budget director, provost, legal director, and nearly all of the deans left the university, for various reasons, ranging from retirement to finding other opportunities. New leadership entered, including the school's first female president. But in that immediate moment, no one praised or thanked me for shining a light on the injustice. My budget was still cut. Scholarship funds were slashed and additional financial aid for students eliminated. Other university officials I reached out to in an effort to share my experiences became distant and indifferent, as though at any moment I would accuse them too of being inappropriate in the workplace.

It's easy to assume speaking the truth will lead to justice, or some sort of positive outcome. We should expect it. Surely, if we have something to say and we say it, people will hear us, allies will come to our aid, and the wrong will be made right.

The reality is that things don't always play out that way. As purposeful warriors we need to understand that reality. Elevating our voices won't always yield the success we believe it will or should.

We must speak out anyway.

Yes, when I spoke out against a culture of harassment and abuse in my workplace, I wasn't heard. I didn't succeed in seeing justice served. Even though as a law dean I held one of the most powerful, influential roles within the university, when I spoke out against blatantly inappropriate behavior, I was met with a subsequent lack of accountability (for him) and negative consequences (for me).

But that's not the end of the story.

Sure, just because no one at the university heard me in that moment, even though this injustice was unchanged despite my speaking out, that didn't mean my voice fell on deaf ears.

First, overcoming my fears about speaking out in and of itself made me stronger. It changed my inner dialogue around what to do, helping me find, and hone, a voice in me that had previously been dormant. After what I'd gone through, I would no longer stand to be treated poorly and would reject—perhaps more quickly next time—abusive behavior. I found power and courage in acting with integrity, even if people didn't respond the way that I'd hoped. That muscle growth would make speaking out again, persistently, into the future, easier every time—such as when, ten years later, I was attacked with lies from the president of the United States.

Second, even when speaking out doesn't instantly change our immediate circumstance, or even temporarily sets us back, it has an inevitable impact beyond that moment. Sure, speaking out against harassment I endured as a young female law dean might have brought little immediate change. But it opened my eyes to so many similar experiences other women were enduring that I hadn't noticed before. And it activated me to do something to help them.

When we stand up for ourselves, and act with courage and integrity as purposeful warriors, we send a powerful message that extends past ourselves. We open the door for others to see themselves in our struggle and empower them to speak out as well.

Me Too

One of the most consequential conversations I've ever had was over lunch with Carolyn Cassin, president of the Michigan Women's Foundation and one of Michigan's most successful female business leaders.

Over her forty-year career Carolyn had launched and led two successful companies while also turning around three others, including a failing hospice organization that she built into the largest and one of the best-run hospices in the country. She shared with me multiple stories from her own life while repeatedly expressing great sadness, shock even, that what had happened to her in the 1970s was still happening to women in my position over forty years later.

"Look," she said to me with a matter-of-fact, no-nonsense tone after I'd wailed about my predicament at Wayne Law, "there will always be people who are going to try to take advantage of you, manipulate you, and yes, abuse you. If it happened to me forty years ago and it's happening to you now, it's always going to happen to women.

"So instead of focusing on your problem and the issue you're experiencing with this guy, think about those who might have experienced this same type of thing throughout their lives. These women have more wisdom, experience, and maybe more authority than you," she explained. "Ask questions, seek counsel, and learn from them."

I nodded. Sage advice.

"Then," Carolyn continued, "turn your attention to the countless women who have less power and experience than you. Think about how they must be suffering with even less help than you. Just like you, they also might not know where to turn or who to trust. Be someone they can turn to and someone they can trust. Listen to their struggle, and use your own platform, wisdom, and experience to help them through it.

"You could sit here all day and focus on yourself and your own problem," Carolyn went on. "But if instead you turn your thoughts and energy to trying to learn from the women 'above' you, who have already experienced much of what you're going through, you'll find you can ask them for help, and I'm sure they'd be more than willing to give it to you.

"Then seek out the women with less power and influence than you and proactively help them navigate the same challenges," she said. "Think about the law students in your school, or administrative staff. I guarantee they may be dealing with the same thing you are, in different ways, and no matter how powerless you may feel in this moment to help yourself, they are feeling even more powerless. Try to help them, even if the people who are supposed to help you aren't doing the same."

I sat there in silence, letting Carolyn's words sink in. She was right. I might not be able to completely remedy my own predicament. But I could be an ally to those with less power or authority than me, to see them, hear them, and help them out. I could be for them the supportive and trustworthy ally that I so desperately needed at the university but couldn't find.

Immediately I began thinking of so many women at the university—staff, professors, executive assistants, students. Were they all going through this too?

"Let's assume they are," Carolyn offered. "What are you going to do about it?"

I returned to the law school with a newfound purpose: helping others find their voice to speak out against abusive behavior in their school, their workplace, or even their home environment. I started hosting lunches with female professors and law students to give them a space to vent and share struggles, and developed a survey for all students to get feedback about their experiences in law school. If others were suffering and I was in a position to help them, I wanted to try.

I shifted the focus away from my specific dilemma and toward the struggle of others, encouraging them to speak out and working to speak out on their behalf. Then something else happened: I began feeling more confident and assured of my own need to speak out about the harassment I was experiencing and try to change it.

In listening to others I found solidarity—and became indignant—through hearing their stories. It helped inform my own efforts to share my experience. So many of us were quietly enduring, in different ways and in varying scenarios, oppressive behavior and disturbing comments that had no place in a workplace, school, or any environment. Behavior and comments that, whether intentional or not, held women back, caused us to doubt our credibility and question our worth.

A few months after my conversation with Carolyn I was speaking to a group of young professionals in Detroit. They wanted to hear about my path to becoming the youngest woman to lead a top-one-hundred law school in American history and what I'd learned along the way. I had a speech prepared that covered the basics—my bio and background, my work and career, how I'd set ambitious goals and worked to achieve them.

But for some reason, when I got up before that group of thirty or forty people, most of whom were women, I decided to tell a different story. I put my prepared remarks back in their folder and instead spontaneously shared what had happened with me and the budget director. I talked about how, even though I'd gone to a women's college and mistakenly thought I was fully prepared to handle any inequality women faced in academia and in the law, I'd found myself completely unprepared and ill-equipped to know what to do when the university budget director started predicating financial allocations on my meeting him for drinks or joining him for a baseball game. I talked honestly about my fears and frustrations, and how hard it was to figure the path forward.

Once I was done, feeling all the cathartic and therapeutic benefits of sharing my story publicly for the first time, a young woman I'd never met before in the back of the room raised her hand.

"That happened to me too," she said.

With a shaky voice that grew in strength as she went along, she began sharing her story of harassment in a publishing company where she worked, and asked for advice on how she should handle her struggle. Before I could answer, another woman's hand shot up, and she immediately began sharing her own story and struggles being the only woman working in a sports management company, dealing with constant verbal abuse and inappropriate behavior from her male colleagues.

I was quick to tell them both I didn't have all the answers. I wasn't sure how they could best work through their respective challenges. But I knew that for me, the first step in that path involved speaking out, with courage, and sharing my story instead of suffering in silence. And that's what the three of us, in that moment, were able to do together.

This was the power unleashed in 2017 as millions of women stood up and said #MeToo, finding solidarity, safety, and strength in each other's shared stories.

The phrase coined by the activist Tarana Burke, in 2006, sparked a movement in 2017 after the actress and advocate Alyssa Milano shared her own story and called on other women who'd experienced sexual harassment and assault to share their stories—or simply say "me too" on social media. Millions of women did so, finding solidarity across countries, industries, and generations. In the years that followed, hundreds of men saw their jobs, roles, and influence diminish as individuals refused to remain silent and spoke their truth about harassment in the workplace.

Speaking out and speaking the truth, these women left victimhood behind and became survivors. They became purposeful warriors, taking back their narrative, demanding to redefine themselves as the heroes of their own stories. That is the power we can all find as purposeful warriors, learning not just to overcome but thrive in response to any challenge, or tragedy, the world brings to our doorstep. It's a power that can only come if we raise our voices and speak up, grounded in truth, courage, and purpose.

Staying Silent

Nothing underscores the need to speak out more than the effect of staying silent.

Because when we choose to stay silent, to not raise our voice to stand up for ourselves, our families, and our greater community, what happens?

Nothing.

Nothing changes. No connections are made. No plans advance. No one learns anything new, no one is inspired to act, no movements occur.

At least in your lane.

But other people will be speaking to fill that void. And their messages may not align with yours. Their purpose may run contrary to yours. They may speak with divisiveness and deceit, bolster corruption or cover-ups, allow harm or injustices to continue or get worse.

Without your voice to counter these other voices, to speak out against them, those contrary voices go unchecked. Things that you oppose, that you feel are wrong, will then flourish in your silence.

Do you want someone else making decisions for you, defining what is possible for your community, your country?

Or do you want to have power—over yourself, your life, and your world?

If we don't stand up for ourselves, telling our stories and speaking out against mistreatment, harassment, or injustice, we abdicate our warrior selves and we lose any possible connection to others who are fighting the same battles. Our silence weakens us, and it weakens others who never get to find strength in hearing our stories.

But when we reject insecurity and fear and speak out with purpose, clarity, integrity, and strength, followed by a tangible plan to see it through, we can have a chance—our only chance—to create a better world for ourselves and others. It's our only real path toward seeing our workplaces—and our lives, or the lives of others—get better. And while in speaking up we may not solve every problem, when we remain silent we allow the voices of division, deception, and injustice to ring out louder than they deserve.

And that is the strength of becoming the purposeful warrior. We are all a part of a larger tapestry. Our actions—our voices—have an impact on that tapestry just as much as our inaction—our silence—does. And when we embrace that truth and act on it, we find not just impact but connection—to each other and to our common humanity.

We find camaraderie. We build a path.

And when we connect through that camaraderie, and walk that path, embracing our common humanity and purpose, we find power.

How to Speak Out in Your Life

While it may seem like simple advice, it can be hard to figure out how or when to stand up for yourself, raise your voice, and speak your truth. Even though doing so is necessary to truly be a warrior in furtherance of your own purpose, the risks and possible negative consequences to speaking out, no matter the subject, are real. How do we know when to say something and when to stay silent?

The first step is to know your truth, what it is that you want to call out, and why it is right or wrong. Who is being treated wrongly? Why is it happening? What do you want to change? Maybe it's a belief that your business could be reaching more customers or that a product needs to be replaced. Or it could be your child who needs boundaries or a spouse who needs to do their share of household duties to align with your expectations and family agreements. Maybe a park needs cleaning in your neighborhood or there's a business that's polluting the air or water in your community. Whatever it is, be clear on what it is you want to shine a light on and why it's important to you that you do so.

Next, figure out who you want to speak the truth to, what you want to say, and how you want to say it. Is it the president of the United States, as it was for me in 2020? Your boss? Your spouse? A colleague or coworker? One person, several people, or a larger group? Prepare notes if you have to or, if you have time, write out what you want to say ahead of time. This will help you stay focused on saying your piece without being sidetracked by their response or other distractions.

After that, determine how you want your truth—and through it, you—to be defined. What do you want to have happen as a result of sharing your voice, vision, or viewpoint? Recognize that the words you say may not have the impact you intend. Think through how the person hearing your words may perceive them, based on their own biases and perspectives. See if you can imagine how someone else might hear your remarks and work to match your delivery with how you hope they'll land.

Finally, after going through this exercise, weigh the cost of staying silent. Will your silence give others the power to define you or the world around you in a way that runs contrary to your values, aspirations, and integrity? If it will, you know you need to speak out. Because you can't allow others to define your truth for you, and if you don't speak out, you'll likely be doing just that. Being clear about the consequences of failing to speak out will help illuminate the importance of raising your voice, despite the risks.

Ultimately, determining whether, when, and how to break your silence boils down to whether doing so helps you stay true to yourself and your values. When you choose to speak out for what's right, regardless of the risk or even the likelihood that people will hear you, you reinforce and strengthen your own commitment to living a life consistent with your highest values and aspirations.

That's what being a purposeful warrior is about—finding your voice, speaking with integrity, and following up what you say with tangible actions. As we speak out more, we become better at it, and others do too. Our individual voices become stronger; the companies we represent or communities we fight for grow in influence, prosperity, and power.

And then our paths as purposeful warriors, as we stand up for others, hold bullies accountable, and express our truth, begin to move mountains.

Chapter 4

Grit and Grace

*When I dare to be powerful, to use my strength
in the service of my vision, then it becomes less
important whether I am afraid.*

—AUDRE LORDE[1]

At the core of the purposeful warrior is a devotion to pursuing your most authentic self. Rooting your vision, views, and aspirations in a sincere commitment to who you are and who you hope to be can unleash a powerful energy as you push to realize your hopes for yourself and your vision for the world around you.

There is so much around us—pressures from social media, expectations from family or authority figures, and others' competing visions—that can combine to distract and deter us from our hopes and our vision. A proliferation of people, images, and stories suggests that changing who we are—looking different, acting like someone else, saying something another way—is a far preferable way to gain a position, earn money, or achieve greatness than being our most genuine selves. This can ring particularly true to women and people of color, who are constantly surrounded with images of people who don't look like us holding positions or accomplishing things that we may hope to achieve.

As purposeful warriors, we can turn down the volume of those other noises and turn up the volume of our own voice. We know that when we succumb to others' visions for our path, we risk losing ourselves. But when we focus on doing things our way, we tap into a fire within that propels us forward with confidence, clarity, and conviction.

Finding the tenacity to do all that takes courage.

Pairing Courage with Empathy

Frequently throughout our lives we find ourselves faced with a choice: Do we advance from a place of strength and courage, or retreat from a place of fear? This choice hits us often when we're championing our own vision, especially if that entails heading into uncharted territory.

The good news is, to grow in any capacity means being willing to do hard things and to welcome challenges as opportunities.

Basing our actions on courage instead of fear empowers us to embrace the unknown with optimism and conquer the unease that comes with breaking the mold. It might mean pushing through that difficult meeting, dealing with the disappointment of others close to us, or accepting criticism, even if it's unwarranted.

Much of what drives our fears are the behavior, views, or reactions of others. We worry about the pain of rejection, the hurt of letting others down, or the anger that can be hurled our way when we fail to meet someone's expectations. That's where grace can enter as a helpful tool.

Grace pushes us to see things from others' point of view and invites understanding when that view doesn't match ours. It helps us see where someone else is coming from, broadens our compassion toward their struggles, and gives us a view into why they may react a certain way to our decisions.

All of that can make it easier to dismantle the fear we might have over a gritty decision, especially if the anxiety around that decision stems from others' potential reaction to our vision.

Practicing empathy also increases our ability to connect to others in a way that can lessen the pain and isolation associated with the risks of speaking out for what we believe in. It protects us from being self-absorbed, which can turn off others and make it difficult to build successful teams.

And it helps us expand our understanding of those around us and why they may harbor certain expectations for themselves, their community, or ourselves. These things all combine to make us more sensitive and attuned to the needs of others.

So while courage helps us stand up for what we believe in, grace gives us a sensitivity to others' plights that will help us overcome our fears with kindness, warmth, and compassion. Pairing them together connects us to our common humanity, even while we stay true to our authentic selves.

Much of America saw this on full display in fall 2020, when Michigan's Governor Gretchen Whitmer had to endure and respond to a very public, though thwarted, kidnapping attempt for her work keeping Michiganders safe during the COVID-19 pandemic.

I had a front-row seat to the events and her response, beginning when I was driving to work one day and talking to Michigan Attorney General Dana Nessel, who, in her role as the state's chief law enforcement officer, always knew about the threats against us long before we did, and was never shy about letting us know what she knew to help us stay protected.

"They're planning to kidnap the governor," she told me.

"*What? Who?*" I asked incredulously.

Yes, indeed, Dana said, going on to explain that thirteen individuals were about to be charged with planning the attempted kidnapping. Their alleged plan was to either abandon the governor in a boat in the middle of Lake Michigan (yes, really) or take her to another state for a trial and execution.

This seems insane, I thought. Kidnap a governor? Abandon her in the middle of a lake?

But wait, that wasn't all, Dana went on. The men had also allegedly discussed plans for a military-style assault on the Michigan state capitol and attacks against the Michigan State Police, her, me, and various others. The plot was a reaction to the governor's lockdown policies during the COVID pandemic, which involved closing schools, gyms, restaurants, and various other places where the deadly airborne virus could easily be spread. They were data-driven restrictions that she'd worked to implement in order to keep Michiganders safe. Ordering them took a lot of courage, and they were met with a great deal of resistance.

A few weeks later, the FBI made the arrests. Most of the suspects were members of the Wolverine Watchmen, a paramilitary militia group based in Michigan. As Attorney General Nessel and other members of law enforcement publicly announced federal charges for conspiring to kidnap a sitting Governor, it felt like the entire nation collectively gasped in disbelief.

Whitmer responded to the arrests with the same authentic grit that she showed when she led the state through the COVID pandemic.

"When I put my hand on the Bible and took the oath of office twenty-two months ago, I knew this job would be hard," she said on the evening of the arrests. "But I'll be honest: I never could have imagined anything like this."

Her response to the plot exuded strength and determination. She wasn't backing down from any fight. Remarkably, though, Whitmer didn't chastise or attack those plotting to harm her. Instead she called on everyone watching to meet these treacherous revelations with grace.

"As your governor," Whitmer said, looking straight into the camera, "I will never stop doing everything in my power to keep you and your family safe. You don't have to agree with me, but I do ask one thing: Never forget that we are all in this together. Let's show a little kindness and a lot more empathy. Let's give one another some grace, and let's take care of each other."[2]

It was a terrifying moment during a year full of them—recognizing our vulnerability as public officials in a moment where some individuals sought to harm us and our families. But it was also a moment during which Whitmer showed the nation how having strength and at the same time showing kindness to those who wrong us can help us navigate through terrifying scenarios without wavering from who we are.

"We are Michiganders," she said as she closed out her remarks. "I know we can get through this. We will get through this. So let's get through it together."

How Grit and Grace Can Help Us Heal

We all know that life involves setbacks and losses. No matter how carefully we plan, there are inevitable, unexpected challenges along the way. Empathy comes in handy when other people cause those twists and turns, because it helps us understand and adjust to their actions without losing sight of our own vision.

And when the setbacks or losses stem from our own actions, it's just as important we have the grit to fight through them and the strength to show grace to ourselves as well.

Motherhood is central to my life, and like many moms, I am the quintessential mama bear warrior when it comes to protecting or defending my kid—just ask any of the other moms who join me in the dugout to cheer, scream, and get mad at the umps during our kids' Little League baseball games! Being a mom to my son, Aiden, is proudly the greatest purpose of my life, and I love every moment I get to spend fighting for him and being a parent.

So when I found out I was pregnant again, a year after Aiden was born, I was thrilled. It was the joyful surprise of my husband, Ryan's, first Father's Day. We'd just celebrated Aiden's first birthday and I was wondering why I was a little plump around my belly.

So I took a pregnancy test. And, well, turns out I was really, really pregnant.

Eight weeks pregnant.

Amid our elation, we were also a little scared—how would we manage to care for two young kids with everything else we had going on, he as the chief development officer for the city of Detroit and I as the CEO of a national nonprofit who was also, by the way, about to launch a statewide political campaign?

We felt afraid and overwhelmed as we struggled to talk through the details and figure out how another child would fit into our lives. I felt like I had just finished giving birth to Aiden. Here we were preparing for baby number two. Could we handle it?

Still, I loved being Aiden's mom. So bring it on, I thought, building up the courage to be a mom of two.

But the following morning, after I made an appointment with my doctor, the worry took hold. How was I going to manage caring for a newborn with everything else going on in my life?

Would others look down on me for being a mom of two young kids while I ran for office to be Michigan's secretary of state? Could I make sure I was devoting enough time to Aiden while also taking care of a newborn? And what about the additional expenses of expanding our family? How would we handle all of that?

Then, later that same afternoon, only twenty-four hours after I'd learned I was eight weeks pregnant, the bleeding began.

I didn't know what it meant at first. A Google search told me it could be normal, no sign of anything bad.

Or it could be the early stages of a miscarriage.

I'm sure it's normal, I thought. It's just a little bleeding.

Then the bleeding got worse overnight.

The following day I shared everything with my doctor as she ran tests and began an ultrasound. She put the image up on the screen and there it was, the familiar image of a fetus, eight weeks along, that I'd tracked so frequently before when I was pregnant with Aiden. I was so happy, and ready. Ready to be a mom again.

And then came the news.

There was no heartbeat.

I didn't understand at first. Did my doctor just say there was no heartbeat . . . yet? The heartbeat would start later maybe? Like at ten or twelve weeks?

No, she explained. There was no heartbeat.

Is it possible the equipment is faulty? I asked her. Should I get a second opinion? I wondered.

You're welcome to, she said with grace. But our machines are really accurate. It will likely not reveal anything different.

I was in shock as she began talking through my options. I could go in for a surgical procedure, she explained, to remove the fetus. Or I could carry it to term for the next seven months and deliver it stillborn. It's also possible, she explained, that your body will expel the fetus on its own. But there was no timeline or sense of when or how that could occur. There was medicine I could take to speed things along and help the pregnancy pass, she offered.

So I could simply carry around my baby with no heartbeat, I thought, or have a surgical procedure, or take medicine to "expel" it from my body.

I don't recall much after that. She gave me some pamphlets to read and told me to call her in a couple of days as I thought through my options.

Gutted and heartbroken, I drove myself home and cried. I was so ready to be a mom of two. And I couldn't believe that wasn't going to happen.

Later that night, as I was rocking my son to bed, the contractions began.

The doctor had explained that passing the fetus naturally would essentially be like giving birth. I'd feel contractions, and ultimately the "tissue," as she said, would be "expelled."

Thankfully, because my doctor had explained to me what to expect, I knew exactly what was happening as the contractions became more intense and more frequent. They lasted throughout the night, until about 4:00 a.m., when the tissue was expelled. That was it, it was over.

I was no longer pregnant.

Nothing can prepare you for the loss of a pregnancy. And any parent who has gone through such a loss, at any stage, will agree that you never fully recover.

But I still had to show up the next day—as a wife, a co-worker, and a mom. I had to put on a brave face as I honestly explained to everyone what had happened. I felt like a failure, as though there was something wrong with me because I'd been physically unable to bring this child to life. I was still reeling from that devastation and disappointment in myself as I endured everyone's sad reactions to my news. I didn't have the answers to a lot of their questions: Will you try for another kid? How is Aiden handling the news? Are you afraid if you get pregnant again that you'll lose the baby again? (Yes, someone actually asked me that.)

Through it all I still had to stand up, dust off, thank them for their condolences and words of support, and keep going.

On the surface, that took grit—both literally, sometimes gritting my teeth, and figuratively, having a gritty spirit underneath. I needed courage to keep my head high and power through the days and weeks following our loss.

I quickly found that I couldn't sincerely project that strength externally as long as I was internally blaming myself for the pregnancy loss. I needed to forgive and show kindness to myself if I was going to be able to manage this challenge. And truly, it was showing grace to myself that helped me find the courage to heal, express my grief, and keep going.

I worked through the pain and power of letting go of that internal shame. I learned to replace it with compassion and maintain an inward dialogue full of the same warmth and love I displayed to my husband and son.

It was challenging, but it gave me even more strength than I could have imagined. Because as I went through that process something else happened. I found feelings of even greater empathy and understanding for those struggling around me than I'd had before. Yes, caring for and serving others had always been central to my work, but dealing with my own heartbreak and loss enabled me to connect to the same emotions in others—many of whom had dealt with immeasurably worse loss and tragedy. I spent time with parents and other caregivers who'd lost a child, with moms hoping to adopt, and with young people in foster care searching for their forever home. I found in those bonds a strength of purpose to help us endure, understanding for what we needed from each other, and a newfound determination to build better health-care systems that will help us all heal from heartbreak.

Seeing the strength and suffering in the faces of those I'd connected with following my miscarriage, and allowing them to see mine, ultimately helped me find a path out of my own grief. Sharing stories, hearing theirs, discussing the common guilt we felt, and learning about all they'd overcome helped me forgive myself for not being able to complete my own pregnancy. I found a path out of my own grief through a greater understanding of the suffering and losses others had faced. I found that I could open my eyes to all I still had to be grateful for—my son, my own health, family, friends, and loved ones—and all that I wanted to help provide for others, including full access to maternal health and wraparound services for all parents.

Uncomfortable Bravery

Practicing empathy and compassion—toward ourselves and others— helps us make bravery our habit in fighting for our ideals. With every bold decision, we build muscle memory to always choose the fearless route. We don't run from what scares us but instead use our fear as an opportunity to get stronger. Every decision becomes a new chance to bolster the purposeful warrior within.

All of this can be really challenging. But just as athletes endure the discomfort of muscle failure to gain strength, so must we all be willing to be uncomfortable to build a pattern of bravery.

When I walked into a classroom as a law professor for the first time, I felt that acute sense of fear and discomfort. Because there I was, twenty-seven years old, two years out of law school, teaching the law to students who certainly expected me to be older.

And then there was the fact that my initial words as a law professor were: "This is a class about race."

Wayne Law hired me to teach election law, education law, and civil rights law. The first class I was asked to teach focused on the growth of federal civil rights protections, legal reforms like the Civil Rights Act, the Voting Rights Act, and the Fair Housing Act that sought to enable and protect the equality of all citizens. That meant diving into America's challenging history of race and the law, like the Jim Crow– era Supreme Court holding in *Plessy v. Ferguson* that endorsed and upheld the legality of segregated "separate but equal" policies. And it also involved studying the midtwentieth-century legal decisions that preceded the era of federal civil rights legislation, leading with *Brown v. Board of Education*, the court ruling that overturned the *Plessy* decision and ended legalized racial segregation in schools. Our class grappled with both ends of this complicated past and finished with a focus on how these future lawyers could play a role in ensuring equality and opportunity for future generations.

I explained this all on that very first day to a group of twenty-four law students, many of whom were the same age as or older than me. In return, the students looked at me with stone-faced skepticism, suspicion, and maybe a bit of bemusement.

The collective unease of the class was palpable. It was a diverse group: a Black male from Detroit in his fifties who had returned to school mid-career to earn a law degree, a twenty-three-year-old Muslim woman, a Latina single mother in her thirties, a young man from Miami whose family were Cuban refugees. It was clear they each wondered what on earth I had to teach them about race.

They were mostly right. And I think we all knew it.

I took a moment to sit in the distress and anxiety of the moment.

Then I found that bravery muscle. And I trudged forward.

Over the course of fifteen weeks, we talked about race and the law. Every day we engaged in uncomfortable, sometimes acrimonious conversations about race, racism, inequity, and the legal and judicial system. For each of us it took courage to share our stories and offer our truth, and empathy to listen, hear, see, and respect each other. We listened, learned, and built trust in that classroom as we read case after case where the law either enabled and justified or dismantled and eradicated racial stratification. Every day we shared stories and explored ideas in a classroom full of people who, with every class session and with each new difficult conversation, became stronger, more connected, more understanding, and more brave. We embraced the discomfort that permeates discussions about racism and historical inequity—and the melding of varying perspectives that emerges from those discussions—and we each learned things about each other, and our country, that we otherwise never would have learned.

Because we were willing to "embrace the suck," as one student who was former military called it, engaging in tough conversations while also trying to understand where everyone else was coming from.

With each subsequent class discussion, week after week, we all got better and better at being vulnerable, honest, and open, overcoming fears that some had of talking about race. Bit by bit, our time together helped us grow into braver people, community members, and stewards of the law.

It was grit that helped us push through the discomfort and stay the course, to not give up even when awkwardness or pain set in. And grace enabled us to see each other, help each other through those moments, and give ourselves the space to learn and grow.

Collectively, our semester-long journey underscored that if we are willing to embrace discomfort, fight through fears, have difficult conversations, listen, and respect each other's differences, it gives us power to travel whatever path or journey we wish. We weren't good on all or any of those strategies on day one of the course, but each time we met we trained ourselves to see uncomfortable discussions as an opportunity to build our bravery, embrace empathy, and yes, study the law.

That meant learning from examples of everyday citizens who welcomed discomfort in order to achieve significant policy and legal victories. Interwoven through court decisions and statutes was a look at how the civil rights movement utilized nonviolent demonstrations to highlight truth and injustice. With courage and compassion, Americans young and old led the way for a nation—and its lawmakers—to confront difficult truths about our past to build a better future. For us, studying their paths helped us think about how to chart our own while seeing a willingness to be uncomfortable as a tactic that would help us effectively pursue our purpose.

When the Empathy of Others Gives Us the Courage to Leap

I loved beginning my career as a law professor with such incredible students and such a memorable course. It took a leap of faith for us all to trust each other at the outset. What started out as an anxiety-laden setting on many fronts became an experience that showed us all how to grow as warriors for our own causes while working through our fears and showing kindness to one another.

Ten years later, those students and our work together echoed in my mind when I was offered an opportunity to leave the law school and enter a new field: sports.

The Ross Initiative in Sports for Equality (RISE) is the brainchild of the Miami Dolphins owner and global business leader Stephen Ross. It was formed in early 2016, shortly after an incident on the Dolphins team in which several players bullied the offensive lineman Jonathan Martin. Ross had hopes that RISE could leverage the unifying power of sports to bring people together and help to heal racial divisions. The creation of RISE was unprecedented: To launch it, he brought together the commissioners of the National Football League (Roger Goodell), the National Basketball Association (Adam Silver), Major League Baseball (Rob Manfred), and the National Hockey League (Gary Bettman). And one day, while I was in New York City interviewing him for the Wayne Law alumni magazine and asking him to make a sizable financial donation (he was an alum), he asked me to leave my deanship to run it.

Thanks, I told him, but I had no desire to leave a solid, established, comfortable position as the dean of our law school. We were starting to rise in the rankings, meeting our goals, recruiting incredible talent, and firing on all cylinders. I felt a responsibility, I explained, to the students, the faculty, and the entire community, to stay the course and serve for the entirety of my contract. And, as a mom of a young child, there was no room in my life to take on a new job that would have me commuting back and forth from Detroit to New York City every week—even one that so uniquely combined my love of sports with my passion for justice and equality.

Think it over, he said, unwilling to accept a no.

I left his office and, my mind spinning, wandered down to a Whole Foods store on the ground floor of the Shops at Columbus Circle to grab lunch. I walked around, picked out some food and headed over to the checkout line, feeling a little dazed and unfocused as I struggled to process this new opportunity and talk myself into rejecting it outright. Suddenly a brightly colored magazine cover caught my eye.

TAKE THE LEAP, it said in big bold letters, teasing an article inside about—yep, you guessed it—having the courage to leave one job for another.

A pesky little voice inside me tugged at my heart to consider the opportunity. Could I be bold enough, I thought to myself, to take this leap of faith onto a less stable path that aligned with my hope to be part of building a world where everyone has the opportunity to succeed?

As the first CEO of RISE I'd build a coalition of sports leaders, athletes, and fans to be champions of racial equality and opportunity for all. The initiative was exciting and necessary, aligning completely with the purpose and fight I wanted to be a part of, and I'd be working on it with the most influential figures in sports.

No, I told myself again. The timing was not right. The sports industry was a totally new environment for me. I was doing great as the dean of Wayne Law; why leave now to jump into a wholly separate world and begin something new?

After lunch I went back upstairs to Stephen's office to tell him thanks, but no thanks. I wasn't going to take the job. Too risky.

I rehearsed my speech as the elevator whisked me more than forty stories up to the top floor of the Time Warner Center. "Thank you for this enormous offer and opportunity," I practiced saying in my head. "I'd love to find a way to make it work, but I love my job as dean, and I just don't think it's going to be possible." Maybe he'd let me join the board of RISE, I thought, so at least I could still be a part of the organization.

I walked back to his office, sat down, and launched into my rehearsed speech.

"Mr. Ross," I began, "thank you for this enormous offer and opportunity. I'd love to find a way to make it work—"

I didn't even get the "but" out before he cut me off. "Terrific!" he said, interrupting and stopping me from saying anything else. Wait, no! I thought to myself. I'm not finished!

Before I could say anything he picked up the phone and called his business partner, Matt Higgins, to take me on a tour of the RISE office headquarters, finalize my contract, and give me information about places to live in New York.

I was stunned into silence. Maybe because deep down I really wanted to take the job, but whatever the reason, I completely lost my ability to speak in that moment.

"There is no one else who can do this job but you, Jocelyn," Stephen said bombastically. "You're going to change the world with RISE. You'll win the Nobel Peace Prize. I can see it now."

He kept talking until Matt showed up, then Matt ushered me out of Stephen's office and down the hall to his to finalize the details.

Then I found my voice again.

"I'm not sure what happened in there," I said to Matt. I couldn't take the job, I told him. I was heading home to Detroit on a flight in a few hours.

"Ooo-K," said Matt, clearly having seen this sort of thing before. "How about we just go see the offices and look at a contract and go from there?" I began to see how he'd earned a reputation as Stephen's "closer."

Matt showed me around what would be my office, complete with a beautiful view of the New York City skyline. He introduced me to several inspiring members of his team, one of whom took me on a tour of potential apartments and presented me with a contract that would double my salary. Then they sent me on my way.

Thanks, I said slowly, gathering all the materials and getting ready to grab an Uber to LaGuardia Airport and catch my flight back home to Detroit.

I landed in Michigan a few hours later with my mind still racing. I walked in a daze through the airport terminal, thinking, Did I just accept a new job? Then I saw a familiar face walking toward me.

It was Margaret Winters, the provost at Wayne State University, my boss at the time.

She greeted me with a hug, telling me she was off to catch a flight. I looked at her sheepishly and told her what had happened, showing her the bag of items I'd received from Stephen and his team. The apartment options for Manhattan, the materials about RISE and my contract, all of it. I told her the entire story of how I'd traveled to New York to meet with Stephen to interview him for our alumni magazine and ask him to make a five-million-dollar gift to the law school. He responded to my ask, I said, with one of his own. And though I'd rejected his job offer (even if he didn't hear me), now I was wondering if maybe I should leave Wayne Law and take the gig.

Provost Winters looked me in the eyes, took my arm, and said, "Take the job. If that is where your heart is calling you to be, we will work out the rest."

I was grateful for her kind words and sincere warmth. Her caring, sympathetic gesture gave me the space I needed to see what I was being called to do—overcome my fear of the unknown and take the leap of faith into a new job.

That evening when I got home I talked about this new opportunity with Ryan. We were about to become new parents. How, I asked him, could we juggle both a new baby and me taking a new job? Wrong question, Ryan said. The better way to look at, he advised, is to ask myself: Who do I want to be? Do I want to be someone who acts from a place of courage? Didn't I strive to "dare to be powerful," to quote Audre Lorde?

As I started looking at the question through that lens, the anxiety I had about stepping off a cliff into a foggy abyss, the unease I felt in leaving a comfortable, safe position to embark on a new journey, began to melt away. In its place I felt confidence and curiosity: What could I learn at this new job, I thought? I started to see all the good that could come from saying yes. There was the impact I could have on promoting equality and fighting for racial justice, the lessons I could glean working with the nation's most prominent and successful sports leaders, and the adventure of spending time working in a new city.

And so I leapt.

It was clear to me as I drove home from the airport that evening that I wanted to learn how to help heal deep divisions in our society, whether they be around who we love, what we look like, or who we worship. Running RISE could be a chance to do that, to lead an effort that would bring people together in a meaningful way. I couldn't allow the lull of comfort and my reluctance to take on the unknown to restrict my freedom to choose a path that would help me grow as a person and as a warrior.

So I took the less comfortable, more difficult path, seizing a new opportunity to do meaningful, impactful, challenging work.

That leap of faith changed my life. And I never regretted it for a moment.

My years at RISE were filled with extraordinary experiences. I built programs to educate, empower, and inspire athletes and sports leaders to stand up to racial hatred and lead their fans to do the same. We registered athletes to vote, empowered them to be engaged in community service, and organized meetings with their members of Congress on policy initiatives. We launched dozens of youth and high school sports leadership programs nationwide that brought athletes together with local law enforcement to build trust, partnerships, and unity. I got to attend nearly every major sporting event, from several Super Bowls to all-star games to the ESPYs to the World Series.

And I saw firsthand the challenges many women encounter in the sports business. I found that sometimes my very presence made others uncomfortable in a male-dominated industry, which taught me that small, strident acts like standing on the sidelines of a professional football game or speaking to a meeting of team owners were critical to changing norms and expectations.

What also stood out to me was how sports executives and athletes regularly took leaps of faith in building teams and developing new game plans. I saw how the best and most productive team cultures would combine grit on the field with grace off the field to achieve success all around. This meant that teams leaned in to discomfort and in some cases even sought it out, so much that "grit" was a frequent buzzword they used to describe their work. At the same time, empathy was a key value coaches and managers used to build community and support between players. They built camaraderie around the concept of grace, particularly when rebuilding after challenging seasons and overcoming unsportsmanlike conduct.

These lessons underscored to me that the best leaders in any industry—from sports to education to nonprofit management to government—find success in combining these seemingly paradoxical approaches.

Allowing Grit and Grace to Guide Our Path

Having grit means having the courage, determination, and discipline to overcome challenges and push through setbacks. We add grace to bring in the empathy, understanding, and compassion that helps us see others, be seen ourselves, build relationships, and, if needed, sidestep those who may try to stand in our way.

Strength and softness. Toughness and kindness. When paired, they empower a warrior to break down any door, fight through any obstacle, overcome fears, build effective teams, and succeed.

Here's a three-step process I've developed to help you make everyday decisions from a place of courage and understanding, building those bravery and empathy muscles together.

First, when you make decisions, ask yourself if you are evaluating your options from a place of fear or a place of courage. It's OK to recognize that fear can be a factor to consider and feel, but don't allow it to overwhelm you. Instead, when making decisions large and small, try to choose the braver—and maybe more challenging—path.

Building that bravery muscle also requires you to take risks that involve leaps of faith on a regular basis. Seek to do one thing every day that requires you to feel a little uncomfortable, and don't shy away from conversations that require you to step outside your comfort zone. Find inspiration in reading stories that celebrate others' courageous decisions, and think about what you'd need to do to be able to take similar actions. Embrace failures, challenges, and setbacks as opportunities to get stronger.

Then bring in the grace. To show grace to others, work to see the world from their vantage point. Genuinely listen. Notice their emotions and try to take in not just their words but the feelings they are trying to share (and perhaps also those they are trying to hide). Strive to be curious, holding back the tendency to judge and instead seeking in good faith to understand where others are coming from.

Finally, have the courage to show yourself grace too. Forgive yourself when you make a misstep. Perfection isn't possible, so allow yourself to mess up and be real. When you feel discouraged or feel you've let yourself down, practice gratitude and make a list of everything you've done that you're proud of—that day, that week, or that year.

Try to make it a daily exercise to find courage and grace in your decisions, interactions, and challenges. Look at your parents, partners, friends, coworkers, children, and everyone you see through the lens of fearlessness and compassion, trying to recognize the great battles they may be fighting that you know nothing about.

Doing this helps you deal with whatever life throws your way with dignity and strength. Along the way you'll grow your power as a purposeful warrior to stand up for yourself, your community, and your world.

PART II

THE PATH OF
THE PURPOSEFUL
WARRIOR

*To build a successful, sustainable path as a
purposeful warrior, you must be innovative, resilient,
and impact driven; channel anger into action; build
a supportive tribe around you. And never give up.*

Chapter 5

If It Ain't Broke,
Fix It Anyway

Complete victory must be continually pursued;
it must be wooed with all of one's might.

—VINCE LOMBARDI[1]

A central part of finding your power as a purposeful warrior involves discovering ways to embrace innovation and push for change. And when something's broken—whether it's a flaw in our kids' education, potholes in the road, or a power grid that failed—it's easy to know that we need to fix it.

It's not so easy to realize we need to fix something that does not appear to be broken.

"If it ain't broke, fix it anyway" is a phrase I learned from a mentor of mine, former NFL Commissioner Paul Tagliabue. Even when it seems everything is going well, he'd tell me, even when things appear "just fine," let's fix it anyway.

It's a concept of continuous improvement. A pattern that involves us questioning and reevaluating our own assumptions. Taking "just fine" and making it better anyway is an approach that spurs us to ask ourselves and those around us, What can we—or I—do better?

"Fix It Anyway"

I met Paul a year into my job running RISE, in October 2017. I was touring the Atlanta Falcons' home stadium about eight months after their epic collapse and loss to the New England Patriots in Super Bowl LI. Throughout the team there was the lingering and palpable heartbreak of failing on the global stage, but they rebounded by opening Mercedes-Benz Stadium, a state-of-the-art new sporting complex.

Paul and his wife, Chan, joined me for the stadium tour. It was a pinch-me moment in a year full of them—for the better part of two decades Paul served as a very influential Commissioner of the National Football League (NFL). And there I was, getting a private tour of a new NFL stadium with him and Tom Garfinkel, CEO and president of the Miami Dolphins. I was awestruck and speechless as we walked the concourse of the stadium, hearing about everything from why food was priced low ("It's the least expensive hot dog in the NFL," Falcons CEO Rich McKay boasted) to the inner workings and design of the stadium's innovative retractable roof.

As we toured I peppered Paul with questions about his work in the NFL. Paul recalled an important meeting early in his tenure as Commissioner, in 1989. It was with the legendary coach Bill Walsh, who had just retired as the successful longtime coach of the San Francisco 49ers.

To many, particularly football's massive and passionate fan base, there was nothing "broken" about the NFL system of hiring coaches and team executives, Paul explained. "Most teams seemed to view the status quo as acceptable and logical."

Yet it was not lost on him that only one head coach in the entire league was Black: the Raiders' head coach, Art Shell. Even more stark was the fact that when Shell was hired, earlier in 1989, he was the league's first Black head coach since Fritz Pollard, who served as a head coach in the league from 1921 to 1926.

Walsh and Tagliabue met to reexamine the seemingly acceptable "unbroken" and "just fine" practices of head-coach hiring in the NFL. They decided to fix them anyway.

Questioning the assumptions behind the current practices of determining a potential coach's qualifications and likelihood of success, Walsh and Tagliabue began to question why all but one of the current coaches were white. Was there something flawed in the seemingly unbroken NFL hiring system that was leading many qualified coaches to be excluded from the hiring process?

They began reevaluating the hiring process to identify ways to develop diverse leadership talent—coaches and team executives—to improve the league and the game they loved. The idea that talented coaching staff were being left on the sidelines because there was no entry for them into the hiring system meant the league, though *fine*, was not excelling in the way it could with a more inclusive coaching tree.

What followed, after several years of development over the course of Paul's tenure, was the creation of a new league policy requiring all teams to interview coaches from diverse backgrounds for all head coach openings. The "Rooney Rule," strategically named after Pittsburgh Steeler's owner Art Rooney, went into effect in 2003. By 2021, twenty of the thirty-two teams in the NFL had hired Black head coaches at some point.

Paul is the first to admit that progress is still too slow in ensuring that talented people from all backgrounds have equal leadership opportunities in sports. And he emphasizes that one single policy or program could never fully accomplish wholesale changes. Instead, during his time as league commissioner, he adhered to the practice of examining and discarding bad assumptions in order to achieve the most progress and innovation and address the most urgent problems.

"If it ain't broke, fix it anyway," he told me.

At the end of our talk in Atlanta that day, I—stepping out of my comfort zone and taking a risk—asked if he would consider joining the RISE board of directors. RISE was dedicated to developing creative ways to engage sports leaders in the work for equality and racial justice. He immediately agreed to join, ultimately ascending to serve as chair of the RISE board.

From then on out, throughout my time leading RISE and even in the months and years after, Paul and I worked together on a near daily basis. He was essential to helping develop programming for RISE and growing the organization to have national impact, with partnerships in nearly every major sports market.

Paul also quickly became a trusted adviser and mentor, willingly and openly sharing all he'd learned in his decades leading the most influential league in professional sports. From him I learned the value and freedom in reexamining our assumptions and doing hard, uncomfortable things—whether building a team, implementing a vision, leading a complex organization, or championing change.

As board chair he would consistently encourage me to surround myself with people who disagreed with me, even if it made me uncomfortable, telling me: "They will make you better."

I'd get a thumbs-up from him when things got challenging: "Have a high tolerance for conflict," he'd say. "It can't be avoided." He helped me learn to embrace conflict within a team as a tool for collaboration and innovation.

And every day, in every meeting, he'd consistently push the board and me as the leader to try new things or reexamine my approaches and practices—even, and especially, when things were working just fine.

"If it ain't broke, fix it anyway," he'd remind me.

The Philosophy of Continuous Improvement

Paul consistently pushed me to recognize and solve problems that weren't apparent—yet. Anytime I'd express a strongly held notion or opinion, he'd respond with a request for me to question and reexamine it. And he repeatedly urged me to proactively seek out differing opinions so I could listen and learn from those with whom I might disagree and find value in dissent and disagreement.

This often was frustrating and seemed counterintuitive. As a leader executing a vision, why should I stop to purposefully critique, question, and reexamine my presumptions and beliefs? It invited uncertainty and a lack of clarity. It slowed me down and seemed inefficient.

But what Tagliabue was pushing me to see, ultimately, was the value in embracing a philosophy of continuous improvement. It wasn't an approach unique to Tagliabue. There's a Japanese business philosophy known as kaizen, which holds that all employees in a business, particularly in manufacturing, should be continuously improving operations and processes. In kaizen, improvement in productivity should be gradual and methodical, and businesses that adopt it as a practice will require everyone to question, reassess, and evaluate approaches, even when they don't appear to be "broken."

One of the benefits of working with someone who repeatedly tells you to take what's working and try to fix it is that it creates space for you to push back and challenge even that assertion. So I asked Paul why, when there are so many things that are broken, we should spend our time looking to fix things that seem to be working fine.

I remember Paul's kind smile in response. Why would we, he asked in reply, take for granted that we already have access to all the information and data about how something is working? Why should we assume we possess an understanding of every perspective?

Of course, Paul was right. Pursuing any goal with vigor and effectiveness requires that we not simply accept things as we see them, but instead critically examine ourselves and our own preconceived notions as we search for solutions to better ourselves and our world. We have to reexamine assumptions, pick apart preconceptions, and listen to those with whom we disagree.

Even when it seems everything is going well, the concept spurs us to ask ourselves and those around us, What can we—or I—do better?

This in turn enables us to identify potential innovations or improvements long before any obvious problems emerge, and commits us to identifying and fixing fallacies in our own thinking so that we can pursue our purpose with greater strength and confidence. As warriors.

Building this habit of questioning ourselves helps us contribute more productively wherever we are and through whatever life throws at us. It puts us in a constant, steady state of improvement—adjusting, adapting, evolving, and growing. After some time, you'll find this habit of constant reexamination provides you with a unique certainty and confidence that you are looking at things from every angle, have a full understanding of the challenges and counterarguments to your position, and as a result find greater clarity and strength of purpose.

To do this, however, you also must commit to being unflinchingly honest—with everyone around you, most importantly yourself. It's in those quiet moments of solitude, if you're honest and upfront with yourself about whatever it is you're trying to reexamine and fix, that you can better see your errors and find your path forward.

As you build that muscle, working to be brutally honest with yourself about your work, your path, your compassion toward others, and your contribution to the world, you'll in turn fuel your ability to be honest with others and increase your ability to be seen as a trustworthy voice—as a parent, friend, coworker, mentor, or leader. All of that combined strengthens your effectiveness as a purposeful warrior. And it reinforces your ability to act consistently from a place of integrity, honesty, and confidence—because you're consistently examining, questioning, and reexamining your own biases and presumptions.

This was how the visionary commissioner of the National Football League built an institution that remains one of the few remaining entities in America people can unite and rally around.

I started applying the concept in my work on a daily basis. I found that this idea of trying to fix something that doesn't seem broken is at the heart of successful entrepreneurship and innovation.

A Path to Innovation

As a vice president for marketing at the National Basketball Association, Saskia Sorrosa loved her job. A wife and the mother of two daughters, she grew up on a farm in Ecuador before successfully rising through the ranks at the NBA, at one point serving as one of the highest-ranking women in all of sports.

She did it while looking for opportunities to make "just fine" better. And she found that taking what isn't broken and fixing it anyway is a path to innovation.

"When business is running smoothly, we think that's the way it's supposed to be, instead of thinking of all the ways it could be better," Saskia said when discussing her time at the NBA. "We tend to focus on the obvious, leaving behind countless opportunities to innovate."[2]

After becoming a mom, Saskia soon saw something else that was working just fine: baby food.

So she decided to "fix it anyway."

"In the entrepreneurial world, we often hear how start-ups fix or find solutions to broken systems," Saskia explained of her decision to launch a new company, Fresh Bellies, to create healthy baby food for new parents. "Most of these companies aren't fixing a category that is inoperable, bankrupt or out of commission. They're not creating a new product from scratch, either. They're simply making an existing— and fully functional—business better."

Leaving a prestigious and highly sought-after position in the sports industry to branch out on her own as a new parent was a bold move. The baby-food industry was a "well-oiled machine." It was "growing, profitable, and looked perfectly fine from the outside," she recalled.

Yet Saskia saw an opportunity to take something that wasn't broken and "fix it anyway." An approach, to her, that is rooted in curiosity. "All those times we wonder what and how something, anything, could be better is when our best ideas are born," she said in describing her launch into entrepreneurship as a small-business owner.

"Innovation rarely, if ever, comes from trying to fix something that is broken."

Saskia dove into a seven-billion-dollar baby food industry that already was thriving. She reexamined the assumption that all was fine and believed she could take what many didn't see as broken and make it better.

Building off her Ecuadorian heritage and palate, she developed innovative food for children made with natural ingredients and zero preservatives. From "Keep Calm and Cardamom" (dried apples seasoned with cardamom) to "Peas and Love" (snap peas and cumin) to "Two to Mango" ("Tangy mango meets sweet basil in this healthy snack that packs an irresistible crunch!"), Fresh Bellies reinvented and reimagined kids' snack foods. After only a few years on the market, it became one of the top-five brands in natural kids' food in the United States, competing with many global companies that had been in the industry a lot longer.

Fresh Bellies was born because Saskia Sorrosa saw a baby food industry that wasn't broken and successfully "fixed it" anyway.

And to launch her company she had to apply that same principle to herself, taking a career that wasn't broken and "fixing it anyway." As a marketing VP for the NBA, she had a thriving career in sports before making the leap into launching her own start-up business as an entrepreneur. It was a big leap—"I went from sitting behind a desk [at the NBA league offices] to standing under a tent at Farmers' Markets," she later told *Forbes*[3]—and a lonely one. As the only Latina in the baby food industry, there were not many role models to lean on or follow.[4]

"There were so many fears," Saskia recalled. "I didn't know anything about commercializing food. I know a lot about marketing. I know a lot about sports and entertainment. I knew nothing about making food commercially at scale. Plus, where were we going to get the money?"[5]

Saskia was honest to herself about her fears. And she pressed forward.

Saskia's story resonates with me not just because she saw an opportunity for innovation and filled a gap the baby food industry and its customers didn't even know was there. Her story is also powerful because she bravely left the kind of comfortable, influential, well paying, exciting position with a sports league—the NBA!—that many spend their entire lives coveting. Her career was far from broken, but she "fixed it anyway." And now she is one of the most successful Latina entrepreneurs in American history, successfully owning and running a multimillion-dollar company.

And as she was birthing Fresh Bellies in 2017, connecting the concept of continuous improvement to innovation, I was down the street at RISE's New York City headquarters grappling with my own possible career leap.

A Path to New Opportunities

The 2016 election marked a seismic shift in American politics. In the months and years that followed, with Donald Trump serving as president and Republicans in control of Congress, we saw the divisions in America grow wider and wider, with many beginning to question the future of our democracy altogether. It was clear to me that our country was in the middle of a political shift. I could see that, in that moment, those willing to defend democracy and preserve our American ideals against rising threats of autocracy stood to determine the future of our country.

Safely ensconced in the sports world at RISE, watching all of this unfold, I was torn. I loved my job as CEO of RISE. I was thriving. And yes, I was comfortable. I got to travel the country, working with every major professional sports league and team. I earned a six-figure salary, expanding our presence beyond New York to Detroit, Atlanta, Los Angeles, San Francisco, and Miami. I regularly attended Super Bowls, Hall of Fame induction ceremonies, and other iconic sporting events alongside league executives and team owners, rubbing elbows with the industry elite.

And I was working on critical issues. Every day we were in the middle of discussions or leading efforts to advance equity, inclusion, and justice. We led voter registration drives at the Super Bowl. We hosted groundbreaking conversations about race with influential athletes and historic sports figures that earned national coverage. I brought several football and basketball heroes to Washington, DC, to meet with US senators and push for criminal justice reform.

It was in so many ways the dream job. Why leave it to . . . run for Michigan secretary of state?

Well, there was Paul Tagliabue's voice in my head: "If it ain't broke, fix it anyway."

As I contemplated taking my leap and running for office, Stephen Ross tried to get me to stay. "Being secretary of state sounds boring," he'd tell me, while offering a raise and other perks if I decided not to run. "No one I know enjoys elected office."

Paul knew I was happy where I was, and he also understood that I was doing just fine in my position. He didn't want me to leave either. And yet, he reminded me with a wink, "If it ain't broke, fix it anyway."

Because rejecting "just fine" and trying to do better, he told me, could open new opportunities I never could have imagined.

Yet running for Michigan secretary of state in 2018 would be a leap into the unknown. I'd have to make plans to leave RISE and spend my remaining months there recruiting and training someone to replace me. Becoming a political candidate would mean spending hours on the phone, earning no money myself but raising money for the campaign. It would mean begging for support from all corners of Michigan while opponents attacked and criticized me in the press and on social media. Instead of traveling the country, I'd spend my days in the car, crisscrossing the state for hours on end, attending political meetings instead of global glitzy sporting events.

If I lost, I'd have no job to return to. If I won, I'd be taking a 75 percent pay cut.

But a purposeful warrior is courageous enough to take the leap of faith, graceful enough to be OK with failure, sidestepping those who try to hold you back, and taking what isn't broke and trying to fix it anyway.

So I took the leap.

It still was no easy decision. Being a warrior with a purpose is rarely about taking the easy path. But it's always about taking the right one.

I struggled with my decision for months. I wanted to build a career and a life as a purposeful warrior, standing up for myself and doing the right thing. That meant looking at where I was working, running a nonprofit in sports, and examining it, honestly, to see whether it was where I truly belonged in that moment.

Going to RISE in 2016 was the right decision at the time. But was staying at RISE in 2018 still the right decision for me? At a time when my country—and my home state of Michigan—was at a turning point, did I belong on the sidelines advising athletes and sports executives? Was I OK working outside the political system as attacks on democracy were on the rise and our American norms and ideals were being upended, when I knew I had a skill set that could help make things better?

I thought back to the foot soldiers who stood at the foot of the Edmund Pettus Bridge in Selma, Alabama, in 1965; about our connectedness; and about the need to stand up to bullies and ensure our democracy functioned so that the powerful but corrupt could be held accountable.

What was right for me in that moment?

I soon realized that what was right for me was to leave RISE and launch a campaign to become Michigan's secretary of state—the state's "chief democracy officer."

Because although I loved my job leading RISE, I wanted to leverage all I had to fight for our American ideals as a nation and as a democracy.

And so in I dove.

That was when I learned that a willingness to leave behind "just fine" for something better aligned with my values opens new opportunities I never could have imagined.

Becoming a Purposeful Warrior for Michigan

Twenty eighteen was a year, the first of several, in which democracy was literally on the ballot in Michigan. Along with my candidacy, there were not one but two citizen-led pro-democracy ballot initiatives that stood to dramatically affect our elections. One sought to amend our state constitution to expand voting rights, modernize voter registration, and establish voting by mail. The other would end gerry-mandering, putting citizens in charge of drawing legislative districts for the state house and for the US Congress.

As secretary of state, if elected, I'd be charged with implementing these pro-democracy changes—and as someone who'd studied and advocated for these reforms as a law professor and policy advocate for the better part of the previous decade, I was ready.

I traveled the state, happily visiting every county and raising more money than any candidate for Michigan secretary of state ever had before (go big or go home, right?). After a yearlong campaign, and managing a challenging path to victory, I was elected as Michigan's forty-third secretary of state in November 2018.

My life was forever changed. Despite the challenges and the risk, I was on solid footing as a purposeful warrior, standing up for myself, my state, and our democracy.

And when I took the oath of office and was sworn in as secretary of state in January 2019, I declared to the crowd: "It is a new day for democracy in the state of Michigan."

I shared with those gathered my commitment I made in Selma to continue the work of the foot soldiers of the voting rights movement from years past. And now, "as your secretary of state," I pledged, "I will work every day to bring that same commitment as our state's chief election officer to protect your vote, your voice, and our democracy."

Fixing the Seemingly Unfixable: Michigan's DMV

I took an oath that day to not only become Michigan's chief election officer. I also became the state's chief motor vehicle officer, in charge of licensing anything and everything that drives on our roads and travels on our lakes.

That meant I now led 131 local Department of Motor Vehicle (DMV) offices throughout Michigan, each charged with the responsibility for testing and licensing drivers and vehicles and overseeing our state's auto dealers and mechanics.

Yes, I now ran the DMV. The poster child of government inefficiency and failure.

That's when I found out making "just fine" better also enables you to fix some things that many people think are unfixable. Because sometimes when things seem unfixable, we accept them as normal and "just fine," not realizing we could make them extraordinary.

I wanted a DMV that worked well, smoothly, efficiently for everyone.

I wanted extraordinary.

Now, to be sure, when I first took office, those DMV offices were not working—and everyone knew it. They were badly broken through years of neglect and lack of oversight. Residents regularly waited three to five hours for the simplest transactions. The DMV needed fixing. Desperately.

Yet to many throughout state government and even many Michiganders, these offices, operating with severely outdated and broken systems, didn't actually need fixing. Most residents accepted the long waits and slow service as just the way things were. I mean, long lines at the DMV were the butt of jokes nationwide, not just in Michigan. No one in government was incentivized to change something that residents and stakeholders had accepted as "just fine." No one was demanding change.

But I wanted to fix it anyway.

Because I knew that making democracy work for everyone in our state meant not just making voting work well. I also had to make government services work well—for everyone. That meant that even if citizens weren't demanding the improvements, even if there weren't loud calls to fix how our offices operated, I still wanted to fix them anyway. Because every single citizen deserves a government that's efficient and effective, just as much as they deserve a vote that's accessible.

My first day on the job, I began a quest to visit every single branch office in our state, all 131 locations, in my first one hundred days in office. And I did.

One by one I visited, spending time with staff, listening to their experiences, talking with customers, taking notes, and collecting data. We couldn't fix what we couldn't measure. So I needed to diagnose and define the problem if I was going to be able to develop and implement a solution.

I looked at the transactions being done in each branch office, the trends, and customer expectations. I spoke with employees about their work environment and found, among other things, that these moms and dads and grandparents and caregivers behind the counter didn't know on any given day when they'd get home because they were obligated to stay until the last customer was served.

I looked to private industry and noticed that banking, energy, and other customer-service-based companies were moving services online. When I took office, 75 percent of customer transactions at our offices were done in person at one of our 131 branches across the state. A mere 25 percent of transactions were done online or through the mail.

I decided to flip that, so the vast majority of transactions with our department would not require an office visit, thus reducing the number of residents who needed to go to an office and reducing wait times for those who did visit in person.

We doubled the number of transactions offered online and at self-service stations so that, whether residents choose to renew their license plates and driver's or boating licenses online, through the mail, or while grocery shopping, they can do their business without even having to visit a branch office. And we implemented a "call ahead" system enabling anyone to schedule their visit to a branch office ahead of time and be seen immediately upon arrival—eliminating the long lines and uncertain wait times. When we were done, every resident could get in and out of our branch offices in an average of twenty minutes or less.

By the end of my first term, we had dramatically reformed the way every resident interacted with our office. Our residents were satisfied and our employees were happy.

The broken, neglected customer service operation at the DMV that I inherited when I took office was now solidly in the "fixed" column.

But I wasn't done.

Office of Innovation and Continuous Improvement

I knew being a purposeful warrior fighting for better government services in our state required me to constantly examine and reexamine our practices, policies, and expectations. I set up a new department within our offices specifically charged with doing just that—the Office of Innovation and Continuous Improvement. I appointed one of my most trusted, experienced team members, Shawn Starkey, to lead it, because I knew he had a penchant for questioning everything and constantly trying to take what wasn't broken and fix it anyway.

Shawn's mission was essentially to build a team who, across our department, would look for things that weren't broken and fix them anyway, on a regular basis.

Shawn followed a basic principle: If we are going to deliver government services efficiently to everyone, we need to be able to meet people where they are, everywhere, throughout the state. That principle applies to everything our department does, from licensing drivers to helping citizens vote.

And it applies to how government directly serves residents.

For our department, we took this literally. Under Shawn's leadership we created and developed seven mobile branch offices and sent them out to communities—urban, rural, suburban, exurban—across the state. These mobile offices travel to senior facilities, libraries, community centers, neighborhood gatherings, homeless shelters, and any other place where people already are gathering. We bring state services directly to the people.

Shawn's team is also able to respond to emerging challenges quickly and efficiently. Like in October 2023, in Southgate, Michigan, tragedy unfolded when a residential center for seniors caught fire and many elderly residents were suddenly displaced. Then my office learned that in evacuating for the fire, many of the residents had to leave the building without taking their identification and other important paperwork like vehicle titles.

We quickly improved our services just for them, bringing a mobile SOS office to where those residents were temporarily housed to make sure that they could all get their new IDs as our way of making government work for everyone.

At the end of the day, that is my job as secretary of state and as a purposeful warrior: to consistently look at our department and fix everything, whether it seems broken or not, and make it all work better for everyone, from the seniors who've lost their housing or just have other needs, to youth in foster care, to individuals in rural areas with minimal internet connectivity, to individuals in urban areas who may have transportation or other issues. I was proud as secretary of state to make all state services work for all of our residents.

How to Find What Seems "Just Fine" and Fix It Anyway

"If it ain't broke, fix it anyway" is a mantra for innovation and opportunity. It's a technique to reexamine our assumptions and look at things through different lenses, all with the goal of making something— government institutions, sports leagues, businesses large and small, the food industry, even ourselves—better.

It's a practice that helps us empower ourselves as purposeful warriors. The essence of applying this principle to your life is to be unwilling to accept "just fine" and to commit to not waiting for a problem to emerge before trying to fix a situation.

You can start by creating your own version of an Office of Innovation and Continuous Improvement"—in your workplace, family, or community, or in your own life. Whatever form it takes, the idea is to question and reevaluate everything: from your social circle to your career to your family patterns to how you sell a product to how you protect your own health. Whatever it is, we can build a structure to help us consistently apply this practice in everything we do.

We can most powerfully and effectively pursue our purpose or passion when we are willing to question and reexamine our assumptions—especially as we learn, grow, and welcome new voices and perspectives into the fold. By doing all those things, committing ourselves to fix what may not seem broken, we become more effective warriors—on behalf of ourselves and any issue, cause, or purpose we fight to advance.

Chapter 6

Finding Purpose
in Your Rage

Find purpose in your rage. . . . Rage
without reason, without a plan, without
direction is just more rage.

—MICHELLE OBAMA[1]

I still remember the rage I felt on the morning of September 11, 2001.
I was in my first week of law school at Harvard.

I had just finished my morning run and was returning home
when I overheard chatter about a plane crash. Instantly I knew something was very wrong.

Soon after, I learned that the first plane had hit the towers.

I walked back to my small apartment feeling a mixture of shock,
fear, and anger. My law school roommate, Ronja, ran up to me. "We're
under attack! We're under attack!" she shouted. I slowly closed the
door behind me.

Without a word, we both made our way to the television set we'd
purchased when we moved in just two weeks earlier. For thirty minutes
we stared at the screen incredulously as horror unfolded in front of us.

Frozen, shocked, terrified, we watched in silence as the worst terrorist attack in history on American soil played out. At about 9:30 a.m., after what seemed like eternity, I heard Ronja say quietly, "We have to go to class."

She was talking about our civil procedure class, taught by the Harvard Law professor and future United States Supreme Court Justice Elena Kagan. Start time was 9:50. You couldn't be late. We'd just met a few times as a class at that point, but we all knew that Kagan had zero tolerance for tardiness. Showing up to class on time meant you were already late—a few minutes beyond that and you might as well not show up at all.

I knew that, we all knew that. But on the morning of September 11, 2001, I didn't care.

"Go ahead to class," I told Ronja, unable to muster any other words or movement. I would meet her there, I told her, and yes, I'd be late.

Five minutes later the South Tower collapsed.

At that point the surreality of the moment was beyond my comprehension. I couldn't stomach anything more. Nothing seemed real. Everything was incomprehensible. One of the Twin Towers, the World Trade Center Twin Towers, a place I'd visited and looked upwards at with awe at just weeks earlier, was gone. Collapsed. Disappeared into a cloud of dust.

My mind shut down. I couldn't process anything other than a distant sense that I was supposed to be in class somewhere. I left the apartment and walked over to Pound Hall, where class had already started. In a daze, I didn't recognize the buildings I passed or the people around me. I followed other students and eventually found myself in Kagan's classroom, where, surreally, class was continuing as if nothing of note was occurring outside.

I couldn't tell you a thing we discussed in the next forty-five minutes. I vividly remember, though, that when class ended at 10:55, a student came in to announce classes were canceled for the rest of the day.

In a fog, I walked up to him and asked if anything else had happened since the South Tower had fallen. The 3L looked at me, shaken, horrified that I didn't know and that he had to tell me.

"The other tower fell too," he said quietly. "The World Trade Center is gone."

I squinted, fighting back tears, stunned and in shock.

"And," he continued, "something happened in Pennsylvania."

"Pennsylvania?" I whispered, barely able to speak. "My parents live in Pennsylvania."

"Would you like to call them?" he asked.

We all were trying to find something, anything, that we could do in that moment to make sense of what was happening and be helpful in the midst of it. Helping me get to a phone was something he—a student I'd never met before and never saw again—could do.

"Yes," I said. "How can I? Where can I call them?" He took my arm and guided me to an office down the hall, where I numbly dialed my parents' number. My mom answered.

My parents lived around sixty miles from the field in Shanksville where Flight 93 had crashed. But in that moment everything was a blur, and nowhere seemed safe. Somehow reaching my parents and hearing their voices provided some sense of normalcy and grounding in a moment where nothing seemed real.

After my parents assured me they and my brother were safe, someone else helped me find my way back to my apartment. I remember looking around and being unable to recognize anything. I had no idea where I was or how to find my own way around. When I returned, Ronja was on the phone with her mom. Her sister worked in the World Trade Center, and though we'd later learn that she had survived, they hadn't heard from her yet.

We spent the rest of the day in our room watching the news while down the street the man who would later become my husband, Ryan Friedrichs, was doing the same on the campus of the Harvard Kennedy School of Government. He was watching the tragedy play out with a hundred fellow students, all in the middle of their orientation for Harvard's Master's in Public Policy program.

In the weeks that followed, as horror and grief turned into rage, America went to war.

The Power of Targeting Rage
Toward a Greater Purpose

For Ryan, the unprovoked attack on American soil that murdered thousands of innocent civilians on September 11, 2001, including a college friend of his named Todd Ouida,[2] planted in his heart a desire to serve in the United States military and share in the burden of war.

In 2011 the United States was nearly ten years into the war in Afghanistan, with no signs of withdrawal on the horizon. Ryan spent that decade in Detroit working on urban planning and civic engagement. Then in December 2009, President Obama, in a speech at West Point, announced his plans to send thirty thousand additional US troops into Afghanistan.[3] The following year, Ryan met Gold Star parents Steve and Judy Gentz on a fifty-four-mile memorial run in honor of their son Captain Joel Gentz, killed in action June 9, 2010, in Afghanistan.[4] This relationship and the friendships Ryan made with veterans and active-duty soldiers over the years convinced him that he saw a small group doing too much for too long on the front lines of Afghanistan. "I just want to carry that load myself," he told me one morning. Were he to enlist and deploy, he felt, someone else would be able to stay home with their family. Leaning into his fear and wanting to be a smart, judicious, and thoughtful warrior, Ryan studied and read and talked to everyone he could. To him it became more and more apparent that the sacrifices borne by those serving in the US Army's airborne infantry in Afghanistan were among the steepest and most deeply felt in the military.

So that's where he decided to go.

On January 11, 2011, Ryan swore an oath to serve as an enlisted airborne infantry soldier in the United States Army. Nearly a decade after the terror of September 11, 2001, his rage reached its purpose. His oath locked him into military service for the next eight years, four of them on active duty followed by four years in the reserves. That meant he could be called up, no questions asked, and deployed into combat zones in Afghanistan or anywhere else, anytime, for the better part of the next decade.

He headed down to Sand Hill in Fort Benning (now renamed Fort Moore), in southern Georgia, for five weeks of intense basic training, followed by "jump school" to prepare him for a tour of duty in the airborne infantry. On September 11, 2011, he boarded a plane to a US Army base in Vicenza, Italy, where he would join the 173rd Airborne Brigade Combat Team. His unit deployed to Afghanistan a few months later, in 2012.

Ryan's years of service in the army forever changed him, as they changed so many in our country who have served. One of only two other soldiers to serve in basic training, jump school, and the 173rd

Airborne Brigade with Ryan was killed in Afghanistan the month after their unit arrived—a good friend, PFC Shane Cantu.[5] Yet the lives he fought to protect during his time in the military—and after, through the veterans he continues to help and support every day—underscore the power and value of finding purpose in our rage.

Anger is important. It's a necessary part of a meaningful life and a useful ingredient in the warrior ethos. But if that anger overwhelms us, we can descend into division and turmoil, and we will find ourselves sinking into an abyss of dysfunction.

Yet rage targeted toward a greater purpose is a powerful and necessary tool. If we can unpack our anger and find a purpose underneath its fire, recognizing its power and channeling it in a purposeful direction, we can leverage its unique strength into a passion that can propel us down a path that we might otherwise not have seen.

Life as a Military Spouse

I will always remember my mixed feelings of nervousness, unease, pride, and worry as I drove to Troy, Michigan, one cold January morning in 2011 to see Ryan take his oath at a small enlistment ceremony in the Detroit suburb. He smiled as he raised his right hand and pledged to "defend the Constitution of the United States against all enemies, foreign and domestic." Afterward we said our farewells alongside dozens of other families. It was beautiful, heart-wrenching, and inspiring all at the same time. We were all saying goodbye to our loved ones, not knowing when or if we would see them again.

How would military service change these young men and women who were leaving behind all they knew and everyone they loved in

Michigan as they boarded a bus headed to basic training in Georgia? The unspoken question—Will they return at all?—hung over us all as we said our goodbyes. It was coupled with an unspoken connection we all felt to each other, rooted in the common sacrifice we were making as families in the name of the country we loved and service we believed in. Every single person leaving had chosen to put their life on the line and forever change the lives of their loved ones because they believed in service and in America. They are the best of us. Watching them say goodbye to their families as Ryan said goodbye to me gave me at once immense gratitude and deep sadness over the price they were paying—for all of us.

After their bus departed, I climbed into my car and prepared to head to work in Detroit, where I was teaching a law class later that afternoon. As I drove, over the next thirty-five minutes, I looked at every other car on the road alongside me. None of them, not a single one, I thought, had any clue of the sacrifice I had just witnessed. None of them were thinking about the families that were torn apart, kids saying goodbye to their dads, moms saying goodbye to their sons, who one by one were, at that moment, farther down the highway on a bus headed to basic training and then, after that, to parts unknown. I was deeply saddened by both my own loss and the loss of others I'd just witnessed, and by the fact that many others around me were completely oblivious to how much others were sacrificing to serve in the military to protect all of us—and our way of life as Americans.

The weeks and months that followed were filled with isolation, anxiety, grief, and anger. Yes, I was surrounded by people I loved, but they had no way to relate to my experience. I had to prepare myself every day for the worst to happen—to hear a knock on the door and have to begin to plan the funeral for my husband. I asked for help and support but found that, aside from offering consoling words and prayers, no one around me had any idea, I felt what I was going through or how to help me through it.

I know there is a lot of celebration, recognition, and honor of our military service members and their families. Rightfully so. And throughout Ryan's active-duty service, we experienced and felt that in many ways. Politicians never fail to mention their service and sacrifice on Veterans and Memorial Day. And most every sporting game recognizes a man or woman who's put their life on the line to serve their country. But the reality for our military family and so many others is that a lot of those expressions of gratitude feel a mile wide and an inch deep. For most of the time in our daily lives, the 0.5 percent of Americans who serve in the active-duty military assume an almost invisible burden, one shared by their spouses and families. Their constant sacrifice—before, during, and after a combat mission or deployment—is all-consuming and life altering. And for most of the decades it spanned, the war in Afghanistan was not front of mind or in the everyday consciousness of the vast majority of civilians. Soldiers are far away; their families are scattered, their aloneness largely unrecognized.

I felt all of that and more while Ryan was overseas. And I was angry about it. How could so many profess support for our military, and then when our service members or their family members need voting assistance or financial support or legal help, it's so hard to find?

Then one evening, I found a glimmer of resolve to channel my own rage and isolation. Reason and logic set in. If I was feeling this pain, this loneliness, this feeling that no one around me could really understand what I was going through or what Ryan was risking, there must be so many others feeling that same way who were invisible to me. Where were they? How could we support each other?

Service members, veterans, and their families are scattered throughout our country, many of us with identical experiences and no connection to each other. Where were these other people like me, I thought—the military spouses, partners, and family members who were aching for camaraderie and a space to share our unique struggles and fears while finding inspiration and strength in each other and a bond over our experiences?

I channeled my frustration over all this into a plan—an opportunity to help other military spouses feel less alone.

A quick Google search for "military spouse," "Michigan," and "support" brought up only one real find . . . a depression study. The University of Michigan was inviting spouses of active-duty service members to weekly brunches for conversation and fellowship to discuss our experiences.

Well, I'm not depressed, I thought. I'm just lonely. I'm aching to find people like me, going through the same experience, to share and lessen the pain of the loss and fears we were living with on a daily basis.

Still, it was something, a glimmer of a community I could find nearby. A few weeks later I went to a meeting.

With a plan.

I wanted to find purpose in my rage, a way to serve others, to help alleviate the grief and pain other military family members might be feeling or to solve some of the legal or financial problems they might be encountering.

Four other military spouses showed up that day to the University of Michigan Depression Center. None of us were depressed. We all were craving community.

We found it in each other—not just in the monthly brunches and weekly trivia nights we began planning immediately after that meeting, but in the formation of the Military Spouses of Michigan, a new association we created to help ourselves and others in our community find support and combat isolation. We celebrated the birthdays and anniversaries that would otherwise go unmarked. Through a partnership with the Wayne Law Veterans clinic we were able to provide free legal advice and representation in civil matters for spouses who needed help with family law, eviction or foreclosure, employment, or consumer issues. We also provided information about education and employment opportunities, and hosted programs on financial literacy.

From social gatherings, potluck dinners, and movie nights to birthday parties and anniversary celebrations, we worked to bring families together and share our experiences in a fun way. And in 2013 we were honored to represent military spouses around the nation in the presidential inauguration parade in Washington, DC.

Despite our different backgrounds, as military spouses we found common ground. They are some of the best, strongest people I have ever met. And as we each experienced our respective losses, successes, career changes, and family tragedies, we built meaningful relationships with each other and our community, united around our desire to comfort each other with one simple truth: You are not alone.

In forming the Military Spouses of Michigan, I used my rage to create an opportunity to serve. And through that purpose I found not just solace, but strength and joy—and community. We all did. Our purpose was rooted in supporting each other, loving each other, and lifting each other up when those in our families who we were committed to supporting were unable to do the same for us. It was a way not only to make sense of our rage and isolation but to develop something positive and beneficial as a result.

Rage as a Tool to Make Things Better

Anger can fuel our fire as warriors, inviting us to develop solutions we never otherwise would have thought of. It can help us take a wrong and resolve to not only make things right but to make things better.

I experienced this a year before the tragedy of 9/11, when the aftermath of the 2000 presidential election reshaped the landscape of our democracy and tore our country apart.

The night of November 7, 2000, I was watching the election returns as a graduate student at Oxford University, in the United Kingdom. I was gathered with fellow Marshall and Rhodes Scholars in a college common room that was also filled with dozens of students from across the world.

I was in the middle of the group, with a huge marker and large sheet of paper, ready to keep track of which state went to which candidate as the results came in. Indiana and Kentucky went first, both to Bush. I wrote the states' names under "Bush" on one easel. Then South Carolina (Bush), Vermont (Gore), Georgia (Bush). Then, at 7:45 p.m. Eastern Standard Time, forty-five minutes after the polls had closed in the Sunshine State, CNN called Florida for Al Gore. ABC, CBS, NBC, Fox News, and the Associated Press all did the same.

A huge cheer erupted from the room. My boyfriend at the time was from Florida, and he loudly and confidently assured everyone that with Florida going to Gore, the election was done. Finished. It was over. Al Gore would be the next president of the United States.

Except that a few commentators on some outlets were reporting surprise over the Florida call. Several precincts in the Florida panhandle hadn't yet closed. Absentee and overseas ballots—a good chunk of votes in a state with a significant military population serving abroad—were just beginning to be counted.

But cheers drowned their voices when, fifteen minutes after the Florida call, all the networks announced that Connecticut, Delaware, Washington, DC, Illinois, Maryland, Massachusetts, and New Jersey had all gone for Gore. I hadn't yet finished writing all those "wins" on the paper tracking Gore's electoral votes when Wolf Blitzer called both Michigan and Pennsylvania for Gore as well.

By 8:30 p.m. Eastern Standard Time on November 7, 2000, the world was assured that Al Gore had won enough electoral college votes to win the presidency.

Cheers and celebration echoed throughout the room, filled with mostly Gore supporters.

"Thanks, everyone, for a fun night!" I shouted as I left the room to go outside with some friends to grab kebabs at a nearby food truck. "Gore won!" I told my friend Ahmed, whose food truck was legendary at Oxford. He cheered, piling on extra fries to celebrate.

About thirty minutes later, we returned to the common room where we had tracked the results all evening. Walking into the room I saw something crossed out on the sheet I'd used to tally the states Gore won. I peered closer.

A big, fat line was drawn through the state of Florida.

Thinking this was a joke, I went up to the board to fix it when my boyfriend grabbed my arm.

CNN had retracted their call, he told me. Florida might not have gone to Gore after all. With that unknown, it was no longer assured that Gore had enough electoral college votes to win.

Confusion erupted—both in my head and throughout the room.

But wait, I thought, surely they were just triple checking to make sure Florida had gone to Gore before reaffirming the call. A few counties in the state were in a separate time zone, so maybe they'd just made a technical error announcing the results before all the polling locations closed. The networks just called it too early, I assured myself, never thinking they were going to ultimately be wrong.

Nevertheless, a little bit of unease set into my stomach as I munched on my fries.

Then we watched as state after state was called for Bush. Utah, Colorado, Idaho, Montana, New Hampshire, Missouri, West Virginia, Nevada, Arkansas, Arizona . . . the list went on and on as one by one, state after state went red.

By midnight EST, Florida was still uncalled. It was now 5:00 a.m. in England. We were all exhausted. Most of the students had left hours ago. I could barely keep my eyes open. Some friends were determined to stay awake until the race was called. I was not one of them. I said my goodbyes and went home to get sleep, confident Al Gore had won Florida, and with that the presidency. It would all be sorted out and clear in the morning, I told myself as I drifted off to sleep.

Two hours later, the networks called Florida for Bush, declaring him, not Gore, the presumptive next president of the United States.

When I woke up the next morning the results in two states—Florida and New Mexico remained unclear. Gore was still leading, with 259 electoral college votes to George Bush's 246. But thirty-three electoral college votes still hung in the balance.

What followed over the next five weeks was a historic, unprecedented battle over hanging and dimpled chads, Florida election rules, suspicious votes in Democratic areas for Pat Buchanan, recounts, and lawsuits.[6] While several notorious characters emerged throughout those weeks, one in particular stood out to me—Florida secretary of state Katherine Harris.

As Florida's chief election official, Secretary Harris was charged with overseeing the election and any subsequent recounts. Under Florida law she was appointed by the governor, who, at the time, was Jeb Bush, brother to presidential candidate George W. Bush.

Secretary Harris certified Bush as the winner of Florida's electoral votes and refused to allow a full recount. Democrats sued to compel a recount in a handful of counties. The Florida Supreme Court rejected Harris's refusal and voted to allow a recount of the contested ballots, and the recount began under the national spotlight. Then the United States Supreme Court voted to end it, siding with Harris.

In January 2001, two independent investigations into the election and review of the paper ballots cast—one for *The Washington Post* and a second for *The Palm Beach Post*—each concluded that Al Gore had actually received more votes than George Bush in Florida. *The Guardian* later confirmed that "if the newly examined votes had been allowed to count in the November election, Mr. Gore would have won Florida's 21 electoral college votes by a narrow majority and he, not Mr. Bush, would be president."[7]

But in no small part because Secretary Harris had delayed and then blocked a recount—a decision that the United States Supreme Court ultimately upheld in *Bush v. Gore*—Bush was declared the winner of Florida and the presidency.

I was outraged. I was furious. And, like so many Americans in that moment observing everything unfold, I felt powerless.

Unlike the 2020 election two decades later, in this election there was actual evidence suggesting that legitimate, valid votes in Florida went uncounted. And had they been counted, those citizens' votes would have changed the outcome of the entire presidential election. Yet Secretary Harris would not allow them to be counted. I was enraged over the injustice of it all, feeling that we as a nation had just witnessed what evidence suggested was an illegitimate election.

That rage did not lessen when Al Gore gracefully conceded the loss so that the country could move on and heal. It did not subside when George W. Bush took the oath of office, delivering a stirring inaugural address that encouraged us to unite as a country in the ideals that "move us beyond our backgrounds, lift us above our interests and teach us what it means" to be Americans.[8] And it did not go away in the years that followed when I worked as a law student with Professor Christopher Edley Jr. to advise Senator Hillary Clinton in her work to enact the Help America Vote Act (HAVA), sweeping federal legislation that sought to make sure that the election irregularities in Florida in 2000 would never recur.

Working to pass HAVA helped me begin to feel a purpose emerge through my rage, a desire not just to make election administration right, but to make it better.

Had the chaos and confusion of the 2000 presidential election never occurred, very real inequities and other problems with our perennially underfunded election infrastructure might have continued undetected and unresolved for years. Yet election reform advocates were able to utilize the trauma over the 2000 election to bring Democrats and Republicans together in support of much-needed changes and improvements to election policy across the country.

Still, I never forgot about Florida secretary of state Katherine Harris. For amidst all the hanging chads and questionable policies, it was never lost on me that one person, one election official, stood in the way of a full, equitable, efficient recount of every Florida ballot. But for her decisions, I believed, the will of the voters of Florida would have been realized and Al Gore would have become president.

My anger over this perceived injustice did not lessen with time. But as I sought to find purpose in it, I was able to propel my rage into change.

Four years later, in 2004, another secretary of state—this time Secretary Kenneth Blackwell in Ohio—failed to put enough voting machines in densely populated areas of the state like Cleveland and Columbus. This led to eight hour wait times in those cities, causing many urban voters to leave without casting their ballots. In yet another closely decided election, administrative decisions again affected the results.

It became clear to me that when it came to ensuring that elections were secure, accessible, accurate, and fair, the secretary of state—the chief election officer in nearly every state—stood to have a significant impact on the health of the democracy, both in their state and nationwide.

I was particularly moved that in most cases voters elected their state's secretary of state, the one official who would have more influence than any other over their voice and vote in every election. And yet most citizens knew little about who their state secretary of state was and the critical role they played. Even I, as someone who'd dedicated my career to voting rights and fair elections, was unaware until I saw in the actions of Florida secretary of state Katherine Harris in that fateful presidential election in 2000 just how truly influential these individual officeholders could be.

In 2006, after two presidential election cycles where the secretary of state in a battleground state made decisions that had a decisive impact on a national election, I decided to channel my frustration into an attempt to make things better.

I began writing a book about state secretaries of state to educate citizens everywhere about what they do and how their decisions impact how we vote and the integrity of our elections. As part of my research, I spent two years interviewing nearly every sitting secretary of state at the time. It was illuminating—the vast majority were fair, skilled, and transparent professionals who were committed to doing their jobs well for every citizen.

My goal in writing the book was to help us all, as voters, realize our power and authority in electing state secretaries of state of both parties who will adhere to the law and oversee an inclusive and secure election process. I didn't expect to find the sitting secretaries so inspirational. I didn't plan on falling in love with the job. But that's exactly how I felt at the conclusion of my final interview for the book. I turned off my tape recorder and turned to then–Ohio Secretary of State Jennifer Brunner. OK, I admitted to her, I'm sold. I want to do this job too. How can I?

Turns out I'd have to run for office to do the job in Michigan. I'd never planned to be a politician—I was a policy nerd and a teacher. I didn't know exactly how I'd raise the money or whether I had a prayer at winning. But I knew I wanted to try, to make the case to Michigan voters that I knew the job, could do it with integrity, and would ensure every voice was heard and every vote counted throughout our state.

I lost that first election (more about that when we talk about perseverance in chapter 9). But I didn't give up, and I subsequently ran and ultimately was elected Michigan's forty-third secretary of state eight years later, in November 2018. That, of course, positioned me two years later, in 2020, to preside over one of the most consequential presidential elections in my lifetime.

Two full decades after the frustration of the 2000 election, I had found and realized a great purpose. A drive carried me through the subsequent years to learn, grow, and prepare so that twenty years later I was overseeing elections in what would be the "Florida" of the 2020 election cycle. And I was able to not just make things right in that instance but to make them better. Unlike Katherine Harris in 2000, I had a chance in 2020 to serve as a secretary of state who would stand up to protect and preserve the will of the people, no matter what risks or threats came my way. The entire trajectory taught me not only to never give up on our hopes and dreams for our lives but also the immense power that can come from using your frustration and channeling it into action.

How to Channel Your Rage into Purpose

Rage can be the strongest emotion there is, stronger even than love. In a time when so many people feel on edge, uncertain, and scared, it can be tempting to allow that anger to consume and divide us.

But we still have a choice. You can keep yourself from drowning in fury and you can resist being drawn into debilitating despair. Instead, take your pain and grief and transform it into a response rooted in strength and power. See setbacks as an opportunity to build back better.

How do we do that? I've developed an approach I call my "lemonade" strategy. This basically is like taking a sour lemon—whatever is triggering our rage—and using it to make lemonade: a greater, sweeter tomorrow.

To begin, embrace your rage. Taste the lemon with all its bitterness. Give yourself permission to be angry and to feel all of the emotions that come with it. Do not dismiss your fury, bury it, or feel shame in it. Instead, see it as your heart, your gut, your instinct, your psyche telling you something is wrong. Spend time with that emotion. Doing so enables you to experience a part of you that is real and raw and worthy of your attention and energy.

But don't stay in that space forever. After spending some time with the anger, invite your head and mind into the situation. Look at the lemon through the lens of logic and facts—why is it so sour? What makes it bitter? Separate yourself, just for a moment, from the emotion you're feeling and think objectively about what happened, what is triggering your rage, and why. If someone has attacked you or tried to discredit something you've said, is there anything about what they're saying that is legitimate or worth learning from? If your community has experienced a great loss, is there anything that can be learned or reclaimed from that loss? Look at the issue with some distance, as though you were picking it up in your hand and turning it around to empirically find and maybe even understand differing viewpoints and perspectives.

Next is to ask: How can we make lemonade out of this lemon? Can we take this negative situation and make it a win? What would overcoming this attack, loss, or challenge entail? Is there a result, or a solution that would help alleviate the pain and take you into a better place?

Finally, make the lemonade. Develop a plan to channel your anger (the bitter taste of that lemon) into positive action that can solve a problem or enable progress (lemonade). Tap into the passion and energy at the root of your rage and channel it into a response that will address the issue at the root of your rage. You might find you've successfully used all the fury to propel you into a better, stronger, more confident place than you were before.

When we master this technique, we can learn to leverage wrath as a tool to make us better.

To this day, the image that stays with me the most from September 11, 2001, is that of the firefighters running down Chambers Street to rescue those trapped in the World Trade Center. They knew it was unlikely they could rescue everyone trapped in the towers or put out the fires that raged before them. But they ran ahead anyway, out of a sense of duty and a purpose.

We must all be willing to run toward the fires in our own lives, serving as warriors who find courage in our anger and channel that into real change. When we do so, we will discover we are able to use our frustration over a wrong to improve the future and emerge out of any challenging time with the strength and resolve to thrive.

Chapter 7

Mission Driven

What counts in life is not the mere fact
that we have lived, it is what difference we
have made to the lives of others.

—NELSON MANDELA[1]

A lot of what we've discussed so far is about how it's challenging, and necessary, to be a purposeful warrior. Because what we do sends ripples to those around us, we each have a responsibility to raise our voices with courage and kindness in order to speak the truth and advance our hopes for the future. When we do that, we leverage our voice, our talents, and our hearts to make things better—for our immediate world and for the world as a whole.

Along the way on that journey we'll encounter rough seas. It helps to have a clear sense of where we are headed and how we know when we've gotten there, a lighthouse of sorts to guide us to our destination.

As we fight through choppy waters, we need some indication that all our work is having an impact. We want our actions, our lives, our work to make a difference and move the needle. That's the purposeful warrior ethos—we don't just fight, we fight with purpose and we fight to win.

What does "winning" look like?

As someone who's been honored with the Presidential Citizens Medal from the president of the United States, the Profile in Courage award from the John F. Kennedy Library, and degrees from great universities, I've come to see that the true test of our impact is not found in accolades, awards, recognition, or other traditional signs of success. Those are conventional wins, of which we may be able to grab one or two—maybe change a policy, earn a degree, win a legal case, or amass some great financial gain.

What sets apart a purposeful warrior is the passion to advance our mission beyond personal achievement or singular victory. Instead, we measure success by the legacy we create—a lasting and sustained impact that outlives us because we make a difference in other people's lives.

We might change the life of someone close to us—a child, a parent, a spouse, a friend—someone we meet once, or someone we may never know.

It could be one person, or a lot of people.

Or we might never fully know the extent of the lives we touch on our path.

We can measure our effect as purposeful warriors through the difference we make in peoples' lives, no matter how many people we influence. Doing so is the best way to ensure our time in the arena is well spent and generates lasting success.

Impacting One Person May Be All That You Need

When I first started teaching, I struggled to know whether I was making an impact.

Day in and day out, I would go to class or write an article, interacting with many smart people, students and educators, along the way. We'd spend time discussing and deconstructing important issues, positions, and legal theories. It was invigorating, fun, and challenging work.

But did any of it matter? I wondered often. Was I making a difference to the world with all these conversations, debates, and hours of research?

My parents were special education teachers, and from them I learned at a very young age how every person, no matter where they live, who their parents are, or what they believe, deserves an equal shot at achieving success and fulfilling their potential. We're all better off, my mom and dad taught me, when everyone has that equal chance to succeed. Collaboration, inclusion, fairness, and access enable us all to collectively excel and go further than we would as individuals.

After growing up in Pittsburgh and spending time in Boston, Alabama, New York, Washington, DC, and London, I found a home in Detroit, where many of my neighbors lacked equal access to education, political power, wealth, and health.

I wanted to change that. But I didn't know how.

I knew all of Michigan would benefit if we could make sure everyone, from the northernmost corners of the Upper Peninsula to the most desolate parts of Detroit, had a full, unfettered, equal opportunity to succeed and live a healthy, prosperous life. I ached to find a way to further that purpose.

At the same time, I wanted my work to be effective, to make a difference. I didn't want to work and work and work and never see any movement on any of the issues I cared about.

How could I know if my actions in Detroit were doing anything to further my purpose? How would I measure my own contribution or find metrics to define my own success? Was it quantified in laws passed? Press conferences held? Student job placements or grades?

There were plenty of measures I could use to evaluate my work, but how could I know whether it was truly making a difference? As I toiled away in Detroit, I needed to know: Was I furthering my purpose or wasting my time?

I initially became a teacher because I believe in education as a pathway for people to have equal opportunity and access—to a well-paying job, good health care, safety, clean air and water, and so many other critical needs that we all deserve to have met, but that can be difficult to manage for many. I wanted everyone to have an equal chance to thrive and prosper in our state. Specifically, as a law professor, I hoped to equip future attorneys training in Detroit with the ability to not just thrive themselves but to help others do that too, through the legal system or policymaking.

But whether we're teachers, assembly-line workers, health-care providers, or electricians, it's easy to spend our days focusing on what's immediately in front of us. And it can be hard to look beyond that day-to-day grind and get a sense of whether we are making any significant difference.

I got some clarity on this one day during my second year teaching when a young law student approached me after class.

We'd just had a robust discussion about racial discrimination and the impact of federal housing policies on residential segregation when one particularly bright and curious law student named Melanie Elturk approached me.

"Professor Benson, I need to tell you something," she said. "Thanks to you, I found my voice."

That was quite a statement, I told her. I happily asked her to tell me more.

Melanie explained she had decided to go to law school because she thought that's what she was supposed to do. She'd spent her life as a high-achieving go-getter. She saw other smart, successful people getting advanced degrees out of college and felt she should too. She entered Wayne State Law School and earned top grades, but still didn't really know what she wanted to do. When she found herself swept up in the rat race of trying to get a prestigious job or internship and earn a high salary, she realized she was focused on "being an achiever and money and prestige and accolades because that's what we were all chasing."

But something inside her, she confessed, was tugging at her.

When Melanie was younger, her dad would take her to protests and rallies. The glimmer she'd felt then of wanting something more grew into a flame that made her want to fight on behalf of the oppressed and empower those who were voiceless.

Law school had dimmed that flame, Melanie explained. Instead of doing public service law, she was planning to work at a corporate law firm that summer. It was, she felt, what everyone expected of her. But it wasn't what she felt called to do.

"Then I took your class," she said. "And now I know I don't want to go into corporate law. I want to fight for the oppressed. I want to elevate the voiceless. I want to make sure everyone has a voice. I want to fight for equality and civil rights. I want to make sure our justice system fulfills the promises in our Constitution. I want to be a civil rights lawyer."

Her eyes lit up as she passionately shared with me how our class discussions of historical and present-day inequality had been illuminating for her. And now she wanted to do something about that inequality. In my class, Melanie found the words and vocabulary to articulate a purpose and passion that "was already in my heart, but dormant," she later told me. Our lessons helped her figure out how to use the tools she already had inside her to make a difference and follow her heart.

After my conversation with Melanie, my goal, a way to evaluate my impact as an educator, crystallized.

I would know if I was making a difference along my path as an educator based on how often I could point to at least one student whose life I'd influenced in a positive way.

It's the "starfish" principle, named after an essay by Loren Eiseley that tells the story of a man walking along the beach who sees a boy picking up starfish and gently throwing them back into the sea.

"Young man, what are you doing?" he asks the boy.

"Throwing starfish back into the ocean," the boy replies. "The surf is up, and the tide is going out. If I don't throw them back, they'll die."

The man laughs and says to the boy, "Do you realize there are miles of miles of beach and hundreds of starfish? You can't make any difference."

The boy then bends down to pick up another starfish and throws it into the surf. He turns to smile at the man. "I made a difference to that one," he says.[2]

The story aligned with my mission as a teacher and educator. Had I made one life a little better as the result of my work? Has at least one student emerged from my classes with a better sense of who they are and what they want to do with their law degree? Did I help a student find their spark and enable them to reject their fears to move courageously in the direction of their own passion or purpose?

Standard methods of evaluating our success as legal educators involve metrics like student evaluations or the number of articles we publish each year. And for good reason. It was important for my students to have strong exam performances or find well-paying jobs with their law degrees.

But after my conversation with Melanie I began to add an additional tool to measure my success: Could I, at the end of every semester, point to at least one or two people whose lives were positively changed for the better because of the work we'd done together? I wanted to be able to make someone else's purpose and path more clear and achievable.

If I could do that, then it could tell me, more than any financial bonuses, awards, or honors, that I was making a difference and advancing my purpose as an educator and as a Detroiter.

Help People First, the Money and Accolades Will Follow

In my years as a teacher I served as part educator, part life adviser. A lot of students would come to me each year to ask for input into their career paths. Often their questions involved whether they should take a safe, comfortable job at a law firm that they were less than excited about. Or should they explore other opportunities that brought with them a little more risk but a lot more personal satisfaction?

Those career advisory sessions always began with me asking them: What is your why? Why did you come here?

Most could quickly rattle off a reason—prosecuting crime, defending the wrongly accused, helping people start their own businesses—and the like.

Then I'd ask them: What would success be to you? What would achieving your "why" look like?

"Putting bad guys behind bars," some would say. How many? I'd ask. "I don't know, a lot," they'd reply. "Enough to get elected attorney general," many would say.

Others wanted to make sure people had a fair defense or wanted to help settle contractual disputes. When I pushed them to get more specific, though, most defined their success through achieving one of three things: affluence, praise, or power.

Large bank accounts, impressive titles, big offices, and prestigious accolades all were things they'd focused on to measure their progress and define their goals along the way. Some sought wealth far beyond what they needed to be financially secure. Many hoped for a title, office, or affiliation with an influential business or law firm. Others, even if they couldn't say it out loud, desperately desired attention or recognition from loved ones and peers. And most were attracted to pathways that would expand their influence, extend their authority, or increase their prestige in their families, communities, the legal or business arenas, and beyond.

Time and time again I would listen as they laid all of this out to me. And after we got that on the table, I'd say to them: Seeking wealth, praise, recognition, and power are all perfectly understandable and relatable goals. But should they be our primary goals?

What, if any, impact can we hope to make beyond these things? Think bigger, I'd implore them. What did they want to have change as a result of their time on earth?

Could they make seeking financial security and fancy titles second in priority to improving the lives of those around them? What would their career and life choices be if they first tried to make a positive difference in other people's lives, and trusted that the other things they desired would follow?

This was the type of thinking, I explained to them, that took me to Detroit.

When I graduated from law school, most of my friends and class-mates went to Washington, DC, New York City, or San Francisco. They landed great jobs at prestigious law firms or positions clerking for high-profile judges.

I moved to Detroit.

Sure I felt the lure to go back to the vibrant, inspiring places I'd lived before to seek out talented colleagues and meaningful work. In New York I'd spent a summer at the NAACP Legal Defense Fund alongside some of our nation's top civil rights attorneys. In Washington I interned at National Public Radio for Nina Totenberg, one of the nation's leading legal journalists. In the United Kingdom I studied at Oxford University as a Marshall Scholar, earning a master's degree alongside future global leaders.

But living in Michigan was inspiring, vibrant, and meaningful too—in a whole other way. First, if I wasn't living in New York or Washington DC, someone else just as qualified or as effective as me would be there in my place, doing similar work and probably having a similar impact.

Could I say the same, though, about Michigan? I wanted to go where my presence made a positive difference in other people's lives. And I wanted to live and invest my time and raise a family in a place where we could earn a living, learn to be gritty and graceful, tough and kind, and do real, meaningful, purposeful work.

I moved to Detroit in 2004 to clerk for Judge Damon Keith, one of the nation's longest-serving federal judges. He was eighty-two years old and had been serving as a federal judge for nearly forty years, appointed by President Lyndon Johnson the same year his friend and colleague Thurgood Marshall was elevated to the United States Supreme Court.

Throughout Judge Keith's time on the bench he'd received dozens of honorary degrees, numerous awards, and other prestigious distinctions. He earned the adulation and admiration of presidents, fellow jurists, and our nation's most prominent civil rights leaders and icons. But he was always focused on helping other people.

As a jurist he never hesitated to speak truth to power, admonishing presidents and demanding equal justice under the law. His decisions blocked President Richard Nixon from engaging in warrantless wiretapping and demanded transparency from the Bush administration, declaring that "democracy dies behind closed doors." He prevented the federal government from infringing on individual liberties, integrated schools and neighborhoods, and helped to battle systemic racism in corporations, municipalities, and schools. His career was devoted to shining a light on and elevating voices impacted by systemic racism and generational poverty. He helped to establish a museum for African American history in the heart of Detroit and spoke out on behalf of men and women left voiceless by a political and economic system that didn't serve or see them.

His life and example taught me that to build longevity as a warrior, you must focus on making a sustainable impact on other people's lives.

The stories he told us as we worked on legal briefs for him were not of the dignitaries he dined with or the medals he received. They were instead of people who would approach him on the street with a story or anecdote about how the judge, in actions he'd taken throughout his life to mentor, uplift, and empower, had helped make their lives a little bit better.

One of his favorite stories to share was of a waiter who approached him once at the Detroit Club, a private lunch club that Judge Keith and several other prominent Black Detroiters frequented. "You probably don't remember me," Judge Keith recalled the restaurant worker taking his order telling him, "but I was in your courtroom once."

The waiter told the judge how he'd been in and out of jail for a lot of his twenties, and one day found himself standing before Judge Keith for sentencing after a jury had found him guilty of a nonviolent crime, his third in as many years. Because he was a repeat offender, Judge Keith could have given him a very long prison sentence. He opted instead, however, to show grace and give him a chance at redemption. Sentencing him to probation instead of prison time, Judge Keith told him, "Get your life in order, son," imploring him to turn his life around and live a more honorable, law-abiding path. The waiter told him that he, as that young defendant, took that advice to heart and rebuilt his life afterward. To that man Judge Keith and his dual mercy and admonishment provided the push he needed to turn his life around. He now was a part-time manager at the prestigious club and was saving up to one day open a restaurant of his own.

Judge Keith was prouder of that story and told it far more often than stories about meeting presidents or getting honorary degrees (though many adorned his office walls). It illustrated how the lives he'd changed mattered far more to him, in his eighties, than any accolade or award. Stories like that, he told us, showed him that his life mattered. Making a difference in someone's life was, to him, the definition of real success.

Judge Keith passed away on the bench in 2019, at the age of ninety-six, just a few days after hearing oral arguments in several cases before the United States Sixth Circuit Court of Appeals. His service as a jurist spanned half a century—fifty-two years—and it was marked not as much by his decisions as by who he was as a person. Humble, kind, honest, he had a character that—in the words of the late US Senator Carl Levin on his passing—"provided timeless reminders of how following a moral path in life can bring fulfillment and joy to those who strive for it."[3]

I told Judge Keith's story over and over to my law students, to drive home the notion that thinking about their career and life in terms of the people they helped instead of the dollars in their bank account would be a better way to seek success and impact as a warrior for justice.

And I also told them about my colleague and friend Bryan Stevenson, one of the nation's most prominent, revered, and respected legal minds.

When You Put People First, Accolades Will Follow

I first met Bryan Stevenson not long after I moved to Alabama in 1998 to work at the Southern Poverty Law Center.

Just a few years earlier he had launched the Equal Justice Initiative (EJI), a small nonprofit legal center dedicated to representing poor defendants on death row. EJI's offices were housed in a nondescript building halfway between a dock on the Alabama River where slaves were once unloaded and Court Square, once one of the largest slave auction sites in the United States.

When Bryan was sixteen, his grandfather was murdered—an event that inspired him to go to law school because he wanted to pursue justice for his family and for others who'd been victimized by gun violence. Then a class on racial inequality in the criminal justice system inspired him to become a defense attorney, specifically representing poor defendants of color in the Southern United States who could not afford quality legal representation.

He moved to Alabama and formed EJI, an organization whose founding mission reflected his own purposeful warrior mission: to eliminate inequities and injustice in mass incarceration and eradicate excessive or wrongful punishment in the American legal system. This mission also included an explicit guarantee of legal representation to every inmate on Alabama's death row.

In the three decades since launching EJI, Bryan built it into one of the most impactful and effective civil rights and legal nonprofits in the country today. And he's built a path for himself as a purposeful warrior.

Bryan did not move to Alabama in search of prestige, praise, power, or recognition. His law office was not glamorous. The work he sought to do—defending poor inmates on death row—was not popular or in vogue.

He moved to follow his passion and fight for other people to receive a fair shake in the criminal justice system.

Bryan saw our common humanity, and, though he was just one person, fought to hold a corrupt criminal justice system accountable. And as the inequities of that legal system became more and more clear to him, he refused to say silent in his mission to challenge racial and economic injustice and call for basic human rights and protections for the most vulnerable people in our society.

He's stayed mission driven for nearly three decades, measuring his impact not in the money he's raised, awards he's received, or speeches he's asked to deliver but in the lives he's changed—and saved—as a result of his work.

One of those lives is Walter McMillian's. Walter was a Black American who was convicted and sentenced to death for the murder of a white woman in Monroeville, Alabama. His trial, in 1988, lasted only a day and a half, with the jury finding him guilty despite evidence that Walter was attending a fish fry at his church eleven miles away at the time of the murder. The judge presiding over the trial then rejected the jury's recommendation for a life sentence, instead sentencing Walter to death.

Bryan took on Walter's case and, after five years, successfully overturned his conviction and sentence, saving Walter's life after showing that the prosecution's witnesses had lied and evidence of Walter's innocence had been kept from the jury. And Bryan has pursued hundreds of similar cases in the years since Walter's exoneration, overturning the convictions of over 135 other innocent death row prisoners and revealing deep inequities in the state and federal criminal justice system.

Even though he never sought the recognition, Bryan has since received numerous awards, medals, trophies, honorary degrees, and other accolades recognizing his work. He was awarded the MacArthur Foundation "genius" grant and the ABA Medal, the American Bar Association's highest honor. He wrote a bestselling memoir, *Just Mercy*, which was adapted for an award-winning movie with the same name. He's raised millions of dollars, enabling him to expand the organization to include a museum and build the nation's only memorial to victims of lynching. He is now one of our country's most sought-after speakers and a prolific writer.

But those accolades and traditional successes do not define his impact as a purposeful warrior. They merely reflect it.

It's the people his work has impacted, the lives that are better because of his work, that drives him, sustains him, and defines his success.

Putting People First
Leads to Prosperity

As I shared these stories, I would see the wheels turn in my students' minds as they recalibrated their goals, plans, and aspirations. In the decades that followed, many of them have found financial success and legal prominence. And many of them have also made a positive difference in others' lives.

After one such conversation in the halls of Wayne Law, my former student Melanie Elturk worked to build an impactful path rooted in helping people. After graduation she spent several years as a civil rights lawyer, diving right into the work and building a meaningful law practice.

But she didn't stop there, because her purpose and passion extended beyond the law. Melanie combined her love of fashion and desire to empower Muslim women to launch her own clothing company: Haute Hijab.

Melanie started Haute Hijab after she noticed a lack of options for hijabs that were stylish and high quality. She sought to make hijabs that were fashionable and comfortable, but with a higher purpose as well. Her mission as a CEO of her own fashion brand focused not solely on money or prestige, but on people, encouraging more Muslim women to embrace the hijab in an authentic and beautiful way that reflected their identity as Muslims.

"For me, it's people first," Melanie explained to the strategic thinker Peter Gould.[4] "People first always. Brand second, work second, product second, people first. Because without the right people, you have nothing—nothing else will work."

Haute Hijab is now one of the most popular hijab fashion brands in the United States. And it's a company Melanie built around the ethos of putting people first—from her employees to the customers they serve— and seeking to impact their lives in a positive, empowering way.

Her mission is not only to run a profitable business that designs and sells fashionable hijabs, but also to empower women and break stereotypes, particularly those associated with being a Muslim woman. She also uses her platform to tell her story as an American Muslim and entrepreneur, sharing insights on staying true to her values while building her brand. Her goal is for Haute Hijab to provide a product that empowers women to feel beautiful and stylish while adhering to their faith. It exemplifies being mission driven, ethical, and strong.

Melanie's people-first ethos enabled her to build Haute Hijab into a multimillion-dollar company and a global brand that is among America's most high-profile, go-to Muslim lifestyle brands. Her success demonstrates that profit, wealth, power, and prestige can all come as a by-product of pursuing purpose as a warrior.

But those things are not the root of her purpose. They are not her "why."

The success of Melanie's mission as a purposeful warrior is rooted in the impact her product and her company have on other people.

In making the hijab mainstream and marketing it as a tool of empowerment and pride, Elturk seeks to both "change the perception of hijab within the greater society" and, "more importantly, within ourselves."

"People need to see us as the incredible mothers and caretakers and doctors and engineers and lawyers and students and teachers that we are as Muslim women," she told me, "and value all that we contribute to this society."

It is encouraging to see the wealth, accolades, and prestige that follow Bryan Stevenson, Damon Keith, Melanie Elturk, and other purposeful warriors, even as those results were ancillary to their primary paths. They did not chase them. Yet they achieved them anyway because they each pursued their purpose as a warrior, and those pursuits had tangible, demonstrable impacts on people.

Melanie Elturk sought empowerment for herself, her employees, her clients, and her customers. Bryan Stevenson pursued liberation and justice for the people he served. Judge Keith fought for greater fairness and freedom for all American citizens.

All of them found success when their purposeful work moved the needle in improving others' lives.

Taking a "People-First" Approach in Your Purposeful Warrior Path

How will you define the success of your path as a purposeful warrior? What will be the guideposts, metrics, or goals that will help you chart and define your own success?

Having impact as a purposeful warrior does not need to exclude wealth, praise, prestige, or power. But those things are tangential to true impact.

When we measure our success as purposeful warriors through the impact we have on people, we can more easily define and build a legacy that truly furthers our purpose.

Ask yourself: Am I closer to who I want to be as a person, am I more courageous, innovative, and empathetic because of my work?

Am I measuring the actions I take or the success of my business not just through the profit I am making but also in how my work or product is improving others' lives?

Has someone's life changed for the better because of me?

Ask yourself these questions on a regular basis—each morning, once a week, at the beginning of every month. Doing so will help shift your thinking beyond your own sphere to the difference you are making in others' lives.

Then evaluate or structure your work through the lens of whether there is one person whose life you have made or will make better each day, week, month, or year. List their names, and write about your impact and whether that impact has changed you too. Then set out to do it again, and fight to make it happen, all in furtherance of your purpose and mission.

When we strive to make a difference in the lives of others, we find success—and true, sustainable impact—on our path as purposeful warriors.

Chapter 8

Build Your Tribe:
The Women from Michigan

We're all that woman from Michigan.

—GRETCHEN WHITMER[1]

Few things in life are as important and influential as the people closest to you.

Whether we intend it or not, the people who surround us have a deep and powerful impact on our lives. Our partners, friends, family, co-workers, and colleagues can hone and reinforce our devotion to our mission or purpose. Or they can take us farther from that path, drain our energy, and sidetrack us. At best they provide strength and support—at worst, distraction and discouragement.

This is all heightened on a purposeful warrior pathway. We know the journey is filled with peaks and valleys, and much can transpire to blow wind in our face. Many factors will combine to deter, distract, or discourage you. Some things may steer you completely off course.

Make sure your people do not.

You need to intentionally surround yourself with a tribe who will have your back and support you, counsel you, and bring out your best.

People who know you, believe in you, and are committed to helping you reach your goals. This takes work. But it yields unrivaled dividends.

Think of it as your own personal board of directors—a group of people will look out for your interests and hold you accountable when you veer off course. It could include mentors, advisers, and friends you know you can rely on for trusted counsel. Or loved ones and family members who help guide you and ensure you stay true to your word. You may even want to include past rivals who might be willing to deliver you some tough advice when you most need to hear it. These will be allies who you can rely on to speak the truth to you even—and especially—when you don't want to hear it.

However you build it, collect a group of people who are committed to helping you acheive your purpose as a warrior. And be open to finding them in the most unlikely of places.

My OG Board Member

I moved to Alabama in 1999 without a lot of money. I was fresh out of college and my parents were public school teachers. There was no historic wealth in my family; I'd taken out loans to pay for my college education. So in addition to the volunteer work I was doing at the Southern Poverty Law Center, I took a waitressing job at a local restaurant.

With one foot in each world, I'd investigate hate crimes by day and after hours would head to the restaurant to take orders, deliver food, bus dishes, and hope to earn enough tips to cover my rent and other bills. It wasn't easy—every day I'd be embroiled in emotionally challenging investigations and then dive directly into the physical challenge of balancing orders and cleaning tables.

In my first week at the restaurant, I met a fellow server named Crystal. She was beautiful and confident—funny, outgoing, vivacious. Diners would come in and request her to be their server, and others working at the restaurant would switch shifts so that they could hang out with her.

She was like the sun—a magnet of warmth. People loved Crystal and loved being around her.

But for me, after spending my days investigating neo-Nazi and white supremacist activities, tracking hate crimes and other atrocities, interacting with Crystal was exhausting. I questioned her authenticity and was suspicious of her seemingly charmed life and unflappable sunny disposition. She bounced around the place like a ray of light, blinding those around her with her cheery persona. She seemed to me to be the epitome of carefree privilege.

Boy, was I wrong.

One evening, about two months into my time working there, I was closing the restaurant with Crystal. It was just her and me, wiping down the tables, mopping the floor, and preparing everything for the next day.

We started talking and I was surprised to quickly learn that Crystal wasn't anything like what I'd judged her to be. Far from living a life of ease and privilege, she was a single mom of a two-year-old girl who took a job waiting tables to make ends meet. Her sunny smile masked the pain of having to recently leave her daughter's father, a physically abusive partner. That was a decision that had left her and her child homeless for a time while she worked multiple jobs to save up enough money to find a small place to rent and cover childcare costs while she was at work. She talked a lot about her strong Christian faith and how that had given her strength to leave her abusive boyfriend, even if it meant having no home. We bonded over our shared faith in God and how that informed everything we did. She invited me over to her home the next day to meet her daughter, Alyssa, and have dinner.

In the months that followed, Crystal became a true, dear friend and a trusted confidante. We hit flea markets together to try to find good deals, formed a weekly Bible study, and laughed about *The Real World* on MTV as it ushered in a new breed of unscripted television shows.

Crystal's generosity and support were extensive and unconditional, and we soon became inseparable.

It was never lost on me how much I'd misjudged her when we first met. Not knowing anything about her I'd labeled her as someone with a seemingly privileged existence by virtue of her looks, confidence, political views, and the smile she showed to the world. Yet it was a smile that hid so much inner turmoil, strife, and pain. Instead of seeing her kindness, strength, and all that she'd fought to overcome to give her daughter a better life, I'd wrongly judged her as superficial and naive.

My friendship with Crystal brought home the adage that yes, you can't judge a book by its cover. And it taught me how we can find the most loyal, trustworthy, and supportive members of our tribe in the unlikeliest of places. Our bond was strengthened and deepened by the understanding of the importance and power of women supporting other women. Despite our different lives—I was a nineteen-year-old fresh out of Wellesley College and she a single mom who hadn't graduated high school—we became a team. We had each other's backs. And we helped each other stay true to our ideals, values, and goals—even when so much in our lives tried to pull us off course.

In the decades since we met, Crystal continues to serve as a critical member of my own personal board of directors. She has always helped keep me focused, not only when I fell deep into the challenging work of investigating hate crimes but also years later as I ventured into the political arena. In my most difficult moments she is always there as a trusted teammate, working with others in my tribe to remind me of my "why" as I enter any new arena or battlefield.

The people in our tribe play a critical role in helping us stay true to our values.

And they can encourage, inspire, and empower us to break barriers, defy expectations, and achieve victories we never thought possible.

Changing the Game: The 2018 Election

My first time running for Michigan secretary of state was in 2010. I was a thirty-three-year-old law professor at the time, fresh off publishing a book on the power of secretaries of state to guard the democratic process. I lost that election (more about that in the next chapter), but I didn't lose my belief that government should work for everyone, and that government officials should work just as hard as everyone else. And I didn't lose my conviction that parts of our political infrastructure—like gerrymandering and a lack of transparency—enable corruption to flourish. Losing an election had no impact on my drive to upend a political system that in many ways bent primarily to serving corporate interests instead of looking out for the needs of everyone.

I had a vision for how to make government more accountable and responsive to the citizens it serves. I had no idea if I could succeed in politics without deviating from that vision. I knew I'd be met with resistance and strong headwinds from deeply entrenched interests on both sides of the aisle and in every direction if I worked to make that vision a reality.

But I very much wanted to try.

I was inspired in part by the premise of *Mr. Smith Goes to Washington*, a Frank Capra film from the 1930s about a young gentleman who is appointed to the United States Senate and sets out to take on government corruption. The film suggests it is possible, but demoralizing and difficult, to hold on to our highest ideals and still succeed in American politics.

I wanted to know that was true.

So eight years after my first attempt, I ran again for secretary of state in 2018. This time I was a little older, a little wiser, and a lot more clear-eyed about the challenge of working to increase the transparency and ethical culture of a political system deeply resistant to that type of change.

What I didn't realize is how much I would need the two women I ran alongside with that year—Gretchen Whitmer, who in 2018 was running for governor, and Dana Nessel, who ran for attorney general—to make that vision a reality.

Gretchen and I sat down for coffee in January 2017. We'd been friends for nearly ten years, a bond first forged when we'd both run for statewide office in 2010. In the years since, pundits had pegged both of us as likely competitors to run for governor in 2018. Only we weren't rivals—we were friends. Gretchen was clearly all in to run for governor. I was completely focused on running for Michigan secretary of state.

I vividly remember our talk. Gretchen shared her hopes and plans to build a winning campaign for governor. Several men were looking at the race too—including Dan Kildee, a wildly popular Democratic congressman from Flint, and Mark Bernstein, an influential Ann Arbor personal injury lawyer with deep pockets and a well-known family name because of the frequent television ads and billboards across the state that touted his law firm.

In that meeting Gretchen and I affirmed our respective plans for

2018 and our determination to have each other's backs as the storm surrounded us in the months ahead.

We both proceeded independently to build our winning efforts. Gretchen's headwinds were notable. As she amassed support and built a sizable war chest, she failed to initially gain the support of the mayor of Detroit, Mike Duggan. In late 2017 Duggan circulated a memo "urging labor unions and Democrats to find a better-known figure to lead the ticket." *The New Yorker* later documented how Duggan "wanted Senator Gary Peters to run," while the venerable United Auto Workers were pushing Kildee to get in. When those leaders both declined, Duggan reached out to Bernstein, inviting him to his mayoral mansion on the Detroit River to watch a University of Michigan basketball game and persuade him to run. Bernstein ultimately declined.[2]

I will never forget the message those efforts sent to women across our state. Here we were, shortly after Donald Trump's election as president, and so many powerful and influential men were trying to stand in Gretchen's way. As a former prosecutor and longtime state legislator who was beloved throughout Michigan, she was a strong, viable candidate for governor and was building a campaign that would be poised to win. Whether it was because they didn't believe she could win or were skeptical that she could do the job (how wrong they were on both fronts), the lack of faith that Duggan and others showed in Gretchen's strong campaign, which was already energizing other women across the state, served to remind and reinforce a signal to women leaders that we'd always need to work a hundred times harder than our male counterparts if we wanted them to see us as leaders and winning candidates for office.

And then they tried to pull me into their narrative.

I was already building a strong campaign for secretary of state when, suddenly, others tried to use that against Gretchen. The argument went something like, surely we can't have more than one woman on the ticket at the same time. Surely a Benson for secretary of state campaign and a Whitmer for governor campaign could not successfully coexist. Surely we couldn't both win—no way Michigan voters would go for two women leading our state. Surely our supporters would ultimately collide at the ballot box—confusing voters and donors alike about who they should vote for, because they surely wouldn't vote for women in two out of the three top executive offices in the state. Or so the chatter went.

Then Dana Nessel entered the scene.

Dana was a well-known Detroit attorney who had worked for over a decade as a local prosecutor before entering private practice to prosecute hate crimes against the LGBT community. She'd come into some recent fame, having just won a landmark legal decision in *DeBoer v. Snyder*, a case that successfully struck down Michigan's ban on same-sex marriage.

But most voters didn't know who she was. Legal victories aside, she'd never run for or held public office before, and now she was launching a statewide campaign to serve as the state's chief law enforcement officer.

I'd known Dana a long time at that point and have to admit, like many folks, I didn't know how seriously to take her candidacy at first. It seemed like an uphill battle for yet another female candidate to enter the fray while there were several other well-known and popular Democratic candidates for attorney general, all men, lining up to fill the seat as well. They included county prosecutors, state lawmakers, and one beloved former US attorney with close ties to former President Barack Obama.

Still Dana ran, undeterred, into the fray. Buoyed by her sense of purpose and devotion, she was determined to speak her mind and win her race because she believed she was the best person to do the job. "The office of the Michigan attorney general has lost its way," she said when she announced. "They aren't fighting for the little guy. They aren't fighting to protect our people against rogue bad actors hurting our most vulnerable."[3]

And now there were three Democratic women running for the top three executive roles in the state.

Throughout 2017 and into 2018, not a day went by when I didn't hear from someone—a supporter, party leader, grassroots activist, reporter, you name it—about how it was simply impossible for them to support all three women. Even though we were not actually running against each other and were candidates for three separate positions.

As two women running for downballot positions, Dana and I were constantly pitted against each other. I'd call people for campaign donations and they'd decline, telling me they were supporting Dana "instead" and therefore couldn't give to me. I'd show up to events and people would become awkward because Dana was already there speaking. We weren't running against each other, I'd remind people. You can support us both. But it didn't matter. It was as if we were competing against each other for the fictitious role of "female executive who isn't the governor, of which there can only be one."

Nevertheless, all three of us charged ahead, irrespective of the chatter and assumptions. Gretchen, ever the professional, always rose above it all and focused on her own race for governor. She consistently dismissed or declined to prognosticate about how two other women running statewide for two separate statewide executive positions might affect her electoral chances. I similarly tried to keep my head down and run my race, crisscrossing Michigan to build support and reminding anyone with the gall to explicitly tell me that there couldn't be more than one woman on the ticket that the Democratic party members at the state convention would ultimately make that call.[4]

Dana took the criticism head-on. She was having none of it. She refused to move out of the way or accept this premise that we were competitors. Instead, she called out the argument for its fallacy, ultimately releasing a tongue-in-cheek video blasting the misogyny behind the criticism.

"We need more women in positions of power, not less," Dana said in a video she posted on social media a few months after launching her campaign.[5] "So when you're choosing Michigan's next attorney general, ask yourself this: Who can you trust most not to show you their penis in a professional setting?" she said, alongside photos of men, including then-President Donald Trump, accused of sexual harassment. "Is it the candidate who doesn't have a penis? I'd say so. Some people would tell you I can't be the Democratic nominee for attorney general here in Michigan because we can't have an all-female ticket for statewide office in 2018. Pundits and insiders are asking, 'Can we afford to have a female governor, a female attorney general, and a female secretary of state?' Well, I read the news, and it has me wondering: Can we afford *not* to?

"Yes, I'm a woman," she said after pledging to not "walk around in a half-open bathrobe" or sexually harass her staff. "That's not a liability. That's an asset."

That video went viral and instantly pushed Dana into the national spotlight, solidifying her candidacy and positioning her to win the Democratic nomination.

Dana, to her credit, was the purposeful warrior we all needed in that moment—"in 2014 we had an all-male ticket," she told *Forbes*, prompting her to want to "scream from the rooftop: 'Why is too many women a problem?'"[6]

Heading into the state Democratic party's convention in the spring of 2018, Michigan had three viable, competitive women running for three separate executive positions. And even though we weren't running against each other, it was hard not to feel that we were being pitted against each other—for financial resources, support, and time. And as three women, we didn't have beef with each other—and to some extent all had friendly histories—but the constant and almost universal chorus among Democratic Party leaders, interest groups, and stakeholders created an assumption that it simply was not possible for all three of us to win.

We each ran strong campaigns. We each rallied the party faithful, raised money, and built a strong, broad-based coalition of support for our respective candidacies. We each were nominated by the members of the Democratic Party, and we each headed to November 2018 with a plan to win our individual races.

And we all won.

In November 2018, Michigan became the only state in the nation to elect three women executives statewide.

We broke barriers, defied expectations, and won, together.

The women of Michigan had arrived.

And our work was just getting started.

Women Supporting Women: 2020

A little over a year into our first terms, Gretchen, Dana, and I worked together to lead Michigan through one of the most challenging times in recent history.

From President Trump separately and viciously attacking all three of us in the same week to standing together as we led the state through the COVID-19 pandemic, we've learned the strength that comes in supporting one another through various battles. We've leaned on one another, emboldened one another, opened doors, made connections, and strengthened our individual paths through working as a team. As a trio we've helped each other break barriers and defy expectations. Together we've encouraged each other when we needed support to help us stay true to our missions. Spent hours on the phone together venting and collaborating. And reminded ourselves of why we signed up to serve to begin with.

The collaboration began before we even took office as we sat down to discuss our teams and strategies for our first hundred days. As the only state in the country with an executive branch led almost entirely by women, we hoped to make this more than a moment and the beginning of a new era. Women still held just 15 percent of board seats at Michigan's one hundred largest companies, and girls playing sports—a proven path to developing future leaders—were receiving fewer opportunities in schools across our state. Gretchen and I decided to launch a task force to bring together local and national leaders in sports and education and make a series of recommendations to expand investments for girls and women in athletics. Dana and I became the first secretary of state and attorney general team to testify together— on anything—before our state legislature, which we proudly did in our joint push to expand government transparency and ethics policies in our state.

As a trio we've collectively learned the unrivaled power women can harness in serving as each other's strongest allies. Our work together is complex and not always in sync; there have been times when we disagreed on state financial disclosure requirements or whether to shift the dates of elections. Through all of it we've remained dear friends and confidantes—bonds that were solidified in 2020.

COVID-19 arrived on March 10, the same day as Michigan's presidential primary—our first statewide election since taking office. It was smooth and successful, and two hours after the polls closed the governor called us to say the first two cases of coronavirus had been reported in Michigan.

The three of us immediately began working as a team to assess how we would adhere to evolving health needs and requirements. Two years earlier Michigan citizens had voted for the right to vote by mail, so my focus was on ensuring our election workers were safely and securely able to deliver and receive ballots remotely, and that every voter knew how to get their ballot, fill it out at home, and return it through the mail or at a local drop box.

Our teamwork and camaraderie flourished, and our solidarity was, well, solid. Attorney General Nessel provided legal analysis and offered critical support. We collectively navigated an entire state government while on lockdown. Sure, we didn't always agree on the path forward—I demanded our May local elections be held as scheduled, while others in the governor's administration wanted to postpone them, for example. But through it all we had each other's backs, in front of the cameras and behind the scenes.

One month into the pandemic, as daily deaths were escalating and fear was mounting, Governor Whitmer issued a strong statement acknowledging the growing crisis and the impact it was having on all of us. She set a tone and expectation for us all of calmness, clarity, and confidence.

"We are living in a difficult time, and the unknown is scary," she said. "We must remain steady. We can't allow fear or panic to guide us. The lives of Michiganders are at stake. We must stay the course to save lives. Stay steady. We're going to get through this together."

I used the same tone in my own remarks, both to my team at the Michigan Department of State and to Michigan's voters. Across the state, we kept our offices open and worked with clerks to make sure elections were held as scheduled. When criticism was hurled our way, we, the women leaders of Michigan, spoke out in support of one another.

"One day, because of Governor Gretchen Whitmer's emergency orders, there will be thousands of people who would have otherwise died who instead will go on to watch their kids graduate from school, have grandchildren, or watch the Lions win the Super Bowl," Dana declared a few weeks into lockdowns that had drawn the ire of many frustrated residents.[7] "They may never understand why they never contracted [COVID-19], or how they managed to survive the pandemic when so many others did not. They may even be bitter with the governor for having been kept from activities which have become such routine, unappreciated parts of life. These people may even choose to take it out on the governor later. Her numbers in the polls might diminish. She may not even win a second term. But if people all around our state do not have their lives cut short and instead go on to rebuild their future in the aftermath of this terrible time, then Governor Whitmer will have done her job. Even if the people she has saved and the lives she's touched don't recognize it or appreciate it. And that's what leadership looks like."

The tone and tenor of the attorney general's statement sent an explicit, unequivocal message: The women leading Michigan were willing to do the right thing, even when it was difficult. And we would stick together.

In her book *Fighting for Our Friendships: The Science and Art of Conflict and Connection in Women's Relationships*, the acclaimed author and educator Danielle Bayard Jackson reinforces the power of female friendships and how important it is for women to stand together and support each other in times of crisis. Building bonds as women, she writes, despite implicit and explicit efforts to pit us against each other, is an "act of resistance to oppressive systems."[8] We build those bonds in three ways, Bayard Jackson suggests: through symmetry, secrecy, and support. These "three affinities of female friendship" form the basis of women being able to work together, trust each other, and have each other's backs.

They perfectly describe the dynamic between Gretchen, Dana, and myself. Over the course of the next year, our tribe faced a common adversary: the coronavirus. There was little daylight between us and near complete symmetry as we talked together day and night about emerging variants, threats, and challenges. Our "secrecy" affinity developed as we formed a "vault" comprised of trust and honesty, knowing we could vent and confide in each other as we encountered similar frustrations and struggles. Through making decisions, sharing perspectives, gathering data and research, and defending our conclusions, we found support. Together, the three of us found solidarity not just in the challenges we overcame together but also in the misogynistic attacks, criticism, and threats we each began to face.

The threats began in April with a protest outside Michigan's state capitol building. Protesters, many openly carrying and even brandishing firearms, demonstrated outside and pushed their way inside the building while lawmakers were in session, to demonstrate their opposition to Governor Whitmer's stay-home order in the initial weeks of the coronavirus pandemic. Armed with guns and hateful imagery—including a Barbie doll hanging from a noose—hundreds of protesters circled the building and attempted to enter the chamber where state lawmakers debated Governor Whitmer's request to extend her emergency powers to combat the coronavirus. In a scene that would play out more violently at the United States Capitol the following January 6, the rioters carried Confederate flags and signs painted with swastikas with slogans like "Tyrants get the rope."

It wasn't long before Trump weighed in.

It began with his attacks on Governor Whitmer. In March 2020 Trump was discussing his administration's actions to protect Americans from the coronavirus when he suddenly said he had a "big problem" with the "woman governor" in Michigan, adding that he asked Vice President Pence not to call "the woman in Michigan."[9] Then came, in May 2020, Trump's Twitter tirade against me, "the rogue Secretary of State," for contacting voters with information about how to vote by mail in the 2020 elections. Two days later came an attack on Nessel, whom he called the "Wacky Do Nothing Attorney General" after she called him out for declining to wear a mask while touring a Ford Motor Company plant in Michigan.[10]

Trump's attacks on us continued through the remaining months of his tenure. And each time he lobbed a tirade our way we experienced an uptick in targeted threats and other violent rhetoric. We responded through increasing our mutual support for each other, publicly and privately. As a result, Trump's attacks brought us closer together.

Throughout the 2020 election cycle we were in constant contact, coordinating everything from our clothes to our speeches, working in tandem to defeat not just Trump but misogyny writ large. *The New York Times* declared that in the battle of "Trump vs. the Women Who Lead Michigan," we were the "not-so-secret weapon in the 2020 election."[11] The *Times* article referenced a call with Whitmer and Democrats around Michigan that captured it perfectly: "We're all that woman from Michigan," she said, "and by the end of this, Donald Trump is going to know not to mess with these women from Michigan."

Trump tried to twist and denigrate what we all knew: The women from Michigan had found their power and were working together to move Michigan forward. As I had experienced so many times in my career at this point, his attacks were based on fear—he tried to tear us down to prevent us from growing.

And that growth—and our power—was about to expand.

The Multiplication Effect: 2022

Part of the reason democracy prevailed in 2020 was because the three of us, Gretchen, Dana and I, worked together so closely and so well. We entered the 2022 midterm election cycle, when we were all up for reelection, as a true team, coordinating our fundraising, campaign strategy, messaging, and one viral photo of the three of us posing as our own version of Charlie's Angels.[12]

We found that the sisterhood we'd forged in the fire of 2020 was solid enough to propel all three of us victoriously across the finish line.

We each won our races with sizable margins—me defeating my opponent by 14 points, the governor winning by 11, and Dana by 9.

Then we multiplied.

In 2022 an abundance of women ran for office in Michigan and won, moving Michigan far along the path to a majority-female legislature. Our success led to more success, including the ascension of Michigan's first female state senate majority leader, Grand Rapids' Winnie Brinks.

One of the best things about getting to serve Michigan as secretary of state is getting to serve with Whitmer and Nessel. The trust and true alliance that emerged taught me just how much further we could go as a team, linking arms and working together. We embolden each other when we need to and we hold each other accountable, reminding ourselves of who we are as so much happens along our respective paths that can otherwise distract from our common missions.

We've been part of one another's tribe and served on one another's respective boards of directors, and we wouldn't be as successful in our work leading Michigan without each other.

Building Your Own Personal Board of Directors

As you move forward and craft your own path as a purposeful warrior, know there will be many things designed—intentionally and unintentionally—to knock you off course and distract or discourage you.

It's imperative you work proactively to surround yourself with the people who will inspire, embolden, and support you along the way, helping you to stay focused on who you are and who you want to be as you stand up for yourself and your community. Find those people and build with them a sanctuary of sorts that you can retreat to when the road becomes rocky. Lean on them for respite when the work makes you weary.

Your tribe, your own personal board of directors, should be just as committed to helping you achieve your mission as a purposeful warrior. In her book, *Building Career Equity*, Jan Torrisi-Mokwa talks about a personal board of directors as a network of individuals who act as independent advisers to you, "just as a company looks to its board for guidance."[13] Your tribe must embrace their duty to help you further your mission, check that your actions align with and further your purpose, and help you adjust or adapt your tactics as you move forward. Whether they are work colleagues, mentors, old friends, a peer, a friend's parent, family, or even a former nemesis, we must be intentional about the people we surround ourselves with. In doing so we build a circle of support committed to helping and directing us through our respective missions.

In addition to Crystal, Gretchen, and Dana, my own board of directors includes friends who've known me for years—like Heaster Wheeler, a former longtime director of the Detroit Branch NAACP, and Elizabeth Welch, who in 2020 was elected to serve as a justice on Michigan's supreme court. They also include mentors and role models, like the late United States Senator Carl Levin. Senator Levin in particular embodied everything I wanted to be as a public servant—bold yet gentle, truthful and empathetic, overprepared and always willing to listen and learn more. He never failed to tell you where he stood and ask probing questions to learn about your perspective. He always put in the work, stayed devoted to his home state of Michigan, and never wavered from his commitment to truth, integrity, and leadership. Working with him to launch an academic center devoted to preserving his legacy—the Levin Center for Oversight Democracy—and co-teach law classes with him in his final years will always be among the greatest experiences of my professional career.

Our board of directors needn't be limited to people. It could include a favorite book, poem, song, or inspiring work of art that reminds us of our central goal. Leonard Cohen's "Democracy" is one of my most-listened-to songs on my phone because I play it every time I feel discouraged. I listened to the speech Rev. Martin Luther King Jr. delivered on the steps of the Montgomery capitol building after the voting rights march from Selma almost daily during the postelection challenges of the 2020 presidential election. Movies and even television series can provide doses of inspiration and remind us of who we want to be—in my case, *Mr. Smith Goes to Washington* or the Disney film *Moana*.

People, pets, works of art, and any other thing that we surround ourselves with can provide a quilt of comfort, encouragement, inspiration, and clarity that we can wrap ourselves in as we walk through valleys on our path as purposeful warriors. When those challenging times threaten to steer us off course, our own personal board of directors helps to recalibrate us, refocus us, and remind us of our mission and our purpose.

You can intentionally reach out and build a board of directors that reflects who you need around you. Along the way, ask yourself: Who do you want to go into battle with? Who will be truthful with you even when you don't want to hear it? Who shares your mission or gets your commitment to your own? Who do you trust to help you stay true to your purpose, even when the inevitable valleys along the way in your journey cause you to want to give up or choose another path?

A few other things to keep in mind. First, your board should not be a monolith. It should not be a direct reflection of you and comprised solely of people who look and think like you. Make it diverse and include people who will push back and tell you no. The leadership and executive coach Melissa Eisler refers to this as enabling "thought conflict," building a board where there are "diverging or conflicting attitudes, understandings, interests, values, ideas, or thought processes." If managed well, she advises, thought conflict among a personal board of directors "can lead to more strategic decisions, innovation, and ultimately stronger results." Eisler also recommends identifying someone "who is at least 15 years older than you" and someone "who is at least 15 years younger than you" to help ensure a generational variance among your group.[14]

As you think through who you might want to invite to serve on your board, envision yourself as the CEO of your own mission. Your quest as a purposeful warrior is to build a network or tribe around you—people who represent a diversity of perspectives, can offer new experiences and insights, and are committed to helping you stay focused on your values and aspirations while encouraging and supporting you along the way. They may be past opponents or even current adversaries, older, younger, far away, or close by. You may dislike them one day or many days. And you can reject their advice if you feel it doesn't reflect or further your purpose.

But above all they must be trustworthy truth tellers. People you can rely on, even if at times you disagree, to honor and perhaps even share your dedication to your mission. People who are committed to having your back. Because your journey as a purposeful warrior, as fulfilling, energizing, and gratifying as it might be, will also be lonely, uncomfortable, and maybe even isolating. When those times come, and they will, it is your board of directors, your tribe, your teammates, who will remind you that you are not alone and that you have a tribe you can count on to ride through the storm by your side.

Chapter 9

Twenty-six Miles
and a Baby on Board

Never give in, never give in, never, never,
never—in nothing, great or small.

—WINSTON CHURCHILL[1]

I saw a lot of things waiting tables at a local Italian restaurant in Montgomery, Alabama. A lot. Breakups over spaghetti Bolognese. Ice cream, cake, and other remnants from kids' birthday celebrations crushed into chairs and floor tiles. Rude treatment from impatient patrons and kind stories from others who understood the challenges of juggling plates of food and multiple orders on a busy Friday night.

The experience that stuck with me the most, though, was the story of my toughest customer. Let's call him Dave.

Dave was a regular. He came in at least once a week, ordered basically the same meal . . . and never tipped his server.

Ever.

My coworkers told me about Dave on day one. During training. No one ever wanted him seated in their section, they explained. So be nice to the greeter or else she will seat him at one of your tables when he comes in, they warned.

Nah, I told them. I'm not afraid of Dave. Seat him in my section, I challenged them. Tomorrow.

Sure enough, they seated Dave in my section on my second day at work.

He was very nice, easy to take care of, and we got along well. I worked so hard to make sure he had everything he needed—kept his drink filled, bread basket full, everything. After he paid for his meal and left, I eagerly ran to his table to check. And yes, true to form, Dave had not left a tip.

I was not deterred.

Keep seating him in my section, I told the restaurant manager. I like a challenge.

For three months I waited on Dave once a week. I was kind, persistent, and determined to get this customer to see my value and, eventually, tip accordingly.

It took three months and more pasta con vongole than I can remember. But eventually we developed such a good rapport that I got up the nerve to give him some good-natured ribbing about his failure to leave a tip for us restaurant workers. "It makes us think you don't like our service," I explained. "It's not even about the money"—though it was, kind of—"it's about saying thanks, and making us feel like you see the work we're putting into making sure you have a good experience here."

Dave looked at me and smiled. "You know," he said in his thick Southern drawl, "I never thought of it that way." He winked and I headed back to the kitchen. When I cleaned his table later that evening I was shocked to find . . . Dave had added a tip to his check.

Yes, it was only 10 percent. But I took it as a win.

From then on out, every time I or anyone else at the restaurant waited on Dave, he'd leave a tip.

For the first three months I waited on him it was demoralizing to work hard and not receive any recognition or thanks. But I didn't let it sway me. Instead, I tried to see the challenge of waiting on Dave as an opportunity to get better at waiting tables in general, a skill that was new to me. I also wanted to build my kindness muscle, making sure he had a good meal and service at the restaurant, despite his lack of appreciation. In trying to prove to Dave that I and other restaurant workers deserved fair compensation for our work, I also got a full glimpse into the insecurity of tipped employees in America (who earn far, far less than minimum wage in most places).

I didn't give up on Dave. And eventually he came around and began to see the importance and value of leaving a tip behind for service workers. Perseverance paid off in this case, and along the way it made me a more resilient, efficient, supportive, and even-keeled teammate for my fellow servers.

I like to think of purposeful warriors as being ready for anything life throws at us. We can embrace curveballs—be they unexpected blessings or challenges—and use them to make us better.

No matter what comes our way, we have full control over how we respond. Though we might lose our footing for an instant, we won't allow confusion in that moment to hold us back or veer us off course. Instead, we press on, choosing courage over fear, integrity over the convenience of the moment, and resilience over surrender.

Setbacks give us the chance to alchemize pain and disappointment into power. When trials come our way, we can train our minds to see them as an opportunity to course correct and make improvements.

Learning how to craft a response to challenges in that way, one that strengthens our resolve and reinforces our commitment to the mission at hand, ultimately makes us more likely to achieve our goal as warriors.

It starts with embracing one mantra: Never. Give. Up.

Running as a Warrior

I started running late in life. I didn't run track in high school or college. I was not a natural athlete of any kind. In the middle of Wellesley's college campus was a beautiful lake. I loved walking around the lake and spending time in the adjoining woods to relieve stress. It wasn't long before I found the added benefit of running around the lake. By the time I graduated I was regularly circling Lake Waban on a three-mile run every morning before class.

When I moved around after college—to Alabama and then to England and then back to Boston—running became a constant through all the change. It was also an efficient way to explore new cities and campuses. Running, even just a few miles at a time, helped me center and focus my thoughts and plans as I adjusted to changing circumstances, jobs, and social networks around me.

Then, my first spring in Michigan, I stumbled upon a story in the *Detroit Free Press* about a long-distance running trail nearby. "Run into Spring," it said, with a captivating photo of a nine-mile trail through the woods. I took the bait and decided to run into spring. Every weekend I headed to the trail with a group of friends, adding a few more miles to my distance each time. First it was five miles, then ten, then twelve, then a full eighteen miles out and back. Each run at a greater distance was a bit uncomfortable, and it was also invigorating.

Because every time I ran, through all the chafing, sore muscles, and wind in my face, I found myself getting stronger, more resilient, and tougher than I'd been before.

Running long distances and pushing my body beyond what I thought were its limits became a metaphor for the life I wanted to live—a warrior running toward a better future.

As I ran more and more, I was energized and growing in confidence. Every obstacle I encountered had something to teach me. Every long run made me stronger.

After two months, I heard about a half marathon along a similar trail in Ann Arbor.

At this point I knew that when it came to running, persevering through discomfort and challenge made me a better, stronger athlete. I wanted to keep going, pushing, and seeing just how far I could go.

I gathered a few coworkers and we signed up to run the half marathon.

The night before, I woke up every few hours, afraid I'd sleep through the starting time. Soon the moment arrived. I took a bus to the starting line and lined up alongside hundreds of far more experienced and confident runners.

Just before the race began, I closed my eyes and imagined myself back on Paint Creek Trail, taking one step after another, leaning into the inevitable fatigue, embracing the discomfort, reminding myself I could do hard things, and remembering all that I had come to love and learn about running. I took it one turn at a time, one mile at a time, embraced each challenging hill, appreciating the power and confidence I found in conquering each tough moment.

Then, in the last mile of the course, finish line in sight, I overheard two runners in front of me talking about the Detroit marathon, its international course into Canada, and its finish line: the fifty-yard line on Ford Field, home of the Detroit Lions.

I was in.

I spent the next six months training every day, running farther and faster every time. The training was equal parts energizing and painful, exhilarating and exhausting, yet each time I rejected the urge to give up and chose instead to persevere I became stronger, fiercer, tougher, and more determined to go that next step.

Every point in the run, every step forward, was a chance to allow challenge and discomfort to make me stronger—physically and mentally. To let go of fears and doubt. To overcome anxiety. To build resilience. To not give up. Those cumulative choices along my path to running a marathon didn't just make a runner out of me.

Running reinforced for me, on a daily basis, the power of perseverance.

Before long I was running marathons twice a year. Each 26.2-mile course was different, brought unique challenges, and taught important lessons. I saw details of all five boroughs in New York City's marathon course, crossed dozens of canals on bridges to complete Venice's scenic race, struggled on cobblestone roads in Rome, carried a (heavy) American flag as part of Team Red, White, and Blue in Austin, Texas, and was inspired by stories of heroism that permeate the Marine Corps Marathon in Washington, DC. In Philadelphia, my plans for running fast and alone were stymied when a fifteen-year-old girl in front of me tripped and fell about five miles in. As I helped her up, she told me she'd never run a marathon before and now, overcome with doubt and a sore arm, wanted to quit. Not on my watch, I said, and committed to running with her the rest of the way. We finished together and I ran my fastest time, a lesson that while I love the solitude of running solo, we go faster and stronger when we go together.

My years as a runner—by 2024 I'd run over thirty marathons—have trained me to physically endure and embrace discomfort as a way to improve, both in running and in life. It reminds me of my vulnerabilities—I begin every race not knowing what obstacles await and am genuinely unsure if I'll cross the finish line. And it reaffirms the truth of uncertainty—it's never lost on me that I don't know what lies ahead on any 26.2-mile course, no matter how much I've prepared.

Even though I have crossed the finish line of every marathon I've run, no matter how many times I start again, I am filled with anxiety and emotion as I confront all of the unknowns ahead of me.

Yet when that starting gun goes off and the race begins, I go forward, one step at a time, leaning in to the fear while the opening lyrics to Eminem's "Lose Yourself" play in my ears and a small voice inside me whispers: Bring it on.

That's how running reminds me of the warrior attitude I want to bring to every battle. It's the spirit of the purposeful warrior. Our mission and our tribe guide us, the energy found in defiance and determination emboldens us, the drive to persevere empowers us to push through peaks and valleys along our route.

Overcoming Obstacles in Our Way

Running also taught me that sometimes we need to recalibrate our goals or set new ones when unexpected obstacles pop up on our path. Yes, staying the course is important. But it's also okay to veer left or right to avoid a pitfall or reframe our end goals as we grow. Doing that can even provide us with a chance to exceed our previous expectations and do more than we previously thought was possible.

That's what I learned the second time I ran Boston.

The Boston Marathon is the world's oldest annual marathon and is widely considered one of the most prestigious road racing events. Qualifying to "run Boston" is the pinnacle acheivement for many long-distance runners. It's a 26.2-mile journey through the suburbs of Boston into the city, a course lined with celebratory crowds on streets filled with history. The only way to run it is by qualifying, which means you have to run a wholly separate marathon in the preceding twelve months and complete it in an extremely short amount of time (between two and a half and four hours, depending on your age and gender). I had qualified and run Boston once before, and it was a grueling multiyear effort. But running the Boston Marathon in 2009 was so iconic, and so much fun, that about two minutes after I crossed the finish line in Copley Square I was determined to qualify and complete it again.

So in May 2015, when I ran the San Diego marathon in a very fast three and a half hours, I was astounded. I'd unexpectedly qualified to run Boston a second time—and boy, I couldn't wait.

Then, four months later, I got another surprise.

I was pregnant.

I was elated and thrilled. My heart filled with excitement and anticipation. I was thirty-eight years old and about to become a mom for the first time. My life would forever change. I would have the honor of loving and guiding the little human growing inside of me through life. I started reading and learning everything I could about pregnancy—what to eat, how much water to drink, what vitamins and supplements to take—and parenting.

Amid all the exhilaration I forgot about Boston.

When I remembered that the marathon was scheduled about six weeks before my due date, I laughed and jettisoned my plans for running Boston. Because I had a new mission—taking care of my baby.

In the days that followed the joyful news, my husband, Ryan, and I made plans to buy a new home and prepare for this new addition to our life.

And I also made plans to, for the first time ever, drop out of a marathon.

I hated the idea of giving up. It was tough, but I thought I had no choice. The Boston Marathon was scheduled for April 15, 2016. At that point I'd be thirty-five weeks along—eight months pregnant. Pregnant women are not even allowed to fly on an airplane without a doctor's note after they reach thirty-six weeks. "So you technically could still fly to and from Boston for the marathon," a little voice inside me said. No, I thought, quickly dismissing the notion. I'd be cutting it way too close and potentially putting myself and my kid in danger.

I drafted a note to the Boston Marathon organizers telling them why I'd be dropping out of the race. But, no matter how many times I tried, I couldn't bring myself to hit send on the message. Something inside of me would not let me give up, drop out, or walk away. I'd never bailed on a marathon before. I wasn't a quitter.

Then my husband got me a book called *The Pregnant Athlete*, which made the case, with plenty of research and data to back it up, that women's bodies require the continued physical activity we were accustomed to before we got pregnant. And around the same time I came across a story about another mom in her mid-thirties, Amy Kiel. Kiel had run and safely completed the Boston Marathon the previous year—in her third trimester. She even had the same due date I did, exactly one year earlier.

Her example, along with stories of several other pregnant runners I was reading about, got me thinking. What if the impossible was actually possible? What if instead of "I can't," I began to think in terms of "What if I could?" What if the timing was not a barrier to running but an opportunity to try to run the most prestigious marathon in the world, the Boston Marathon, eight months pregnant?

Seeing that another mom to be had completed the same race I aspired to run, and reading about other women who had kept their running regime while pregnant, gave me hope and cause to believe that I could do it too. The power and inspiration we get through seeing others' examples and the ability they give us to envision what is possible also got me thinking about the example I was setting to those around me. What if I could also show other women that, with attention to health and the advice of a doctor, running a marathon eight months into your pregnancy was doable? Did I have a responsibility to try?

As I was trying to reconcile the joy of my pregnancy with my commitment and goal to run an iconic marathon, the path ahead was uncertain. But I wanted to find a way to go forward because I wanted to live my life making deliberate, intentional decisions to not give up, to persevere.

I want to be someone who sets my own limits and charts my own path. To be brave and not deterred by fears and worry. I want to ask "what if" and "why not" instead of stopping at "it would be difficult" or "it's hard" or "it's impossible."

I want to do hard things.

True, my pregnancy was a curveball in my plans to run Boston. A beautiful blessing to be sure, and also a curveball. I was met with a choice, as a future mom, to persevere and run Boston, or give up and forfeit the race.

Yes, there were legitimate health issues to consider, and those I could and did resolve with my doctor. Beyond that, the root issues behind the choice of whether to run the race or quit were tied to a larger question: Who did I want to be in moments like this, when unexpected developments infringed on my path?

I wanted to be resilient, to adjust and adapt and stay the course. That's what the purposeful warriors in my life all did. That's what I wanted to do as well.

So much of life is a series of curveballs thrown into our best-laid plans.

Disappointments, failures, losses, and surprises constantly conspire to throw us off course and distract us from our own purpose and aspirations.

And deter us they can—but only if we let them.

Because we always have the power to make a conscious choice to persevere and to embrace any obstacles as an opportunity to build strength and resilience.

Instead of fearing the curveballs, what if we saw them as a necessary part of our journey? What if we welcomed what they teach and absorbed their lessons as we keep walking our paths with persistence and perseverance?

In much the same way that the best athletes see loss and setbacks as an opportunity to come back stronger, we as purposeful warriors can see our own challenges as an opportunity to become better and more effective fighters for the issues we care about.

When I looked at the Boston Marathon decision through that lens, the choice was clear. I would address any health considerations, research how other pregnant athletes trained for physical challenges, and not give up. I would run the race.

Perseverance, after all, is ultimately about having hope. It's about believing we can, and hoping we will, succeed in our mission. My mission in that moment was to try to run as much of the Boston Marathon as I could and then safely deliver a healthy baby six weeks later. I didn't know if I would achieve that goal. But I decided to have hope that I would.

Choosing Hope

I spent the next seven months training and, with the blessing of my doctor, flew to Boston in April 2016 to run.

I run a couple of marathons each year and had run Boston a few years earlier, so I had some idea of what to expect on race day. I was nervous but still ready to put one foot in front of the other and see how far along the course I could go. My husband rented a bike and left early in the morning to head to the start line as he prepared to ride alongside me throughout the entire race, with my doctors on call if needed. Of course, I hoped I'd be able to finish, but I didn't know if I could, so I told myself however far I went, however many miles I'd be able to get through, would be a win.

At 10:00 a.m. I stepped off the starting line in Hopkinton and ran the entire 26.2 miles to Boston, one step at a time. Every mile I passed, I told myself, "Now I can always say I ran ___ miles of the Boston marathon while eight months pregnant." Along the journey I took frequent bathroom breaks and ran by a whole lot of folks cheering me on—including a particularly noisy "scream tunnel" at Wellesley College, the halfway point of the race.

Six hours after starting, I saw the CITGO sign that famously signified we were close to the end of the run. I looked to my left and saw an eighty-year-old man I'd met while warming up at the beginning of the race. We looked at each other and smiled, realizing that we were both on the cusp of accomplishing what we didn't think was possible for ourselves just a few hours earlier. I felt absolute euphoria as I approached the finish line and began to realize, for the first time, I might actually do this.

I crossed that final marker and ran into my husband's arms, finisher's medal in hand. I remember thinking, Wow, I did it. I didn't think I could do this and I did. I can do hard things.

On my way back to my hotel for a well-earned rest and carbo-load, I started to wonder about other times when I thought I was bound to limits or barriers that were merely self-imposed. Instead of accepting things outside of our control as things that make us the victim of circumstance, what if we embraced them as an opportunity to raise the bar? Can we redefine our limits and set our own expectations for excellence?

What if we seize the chance to become the hero of our own story, the champion of our mission?

When I lost my first election for secretary of state, in 2010, the habits of perseverance and resiliency I had nurtured as an athlete helped me to pick myself up and choose to run a second time, in 2018. After eight years I came back stronger and more experienced. And I won.

When my relationships fail or disappoint, the experiences I've had as a marathoner, falling down only to get back up again and finish the race, give me hope that I can find or restore love again. When the president of the United States attacked me for simply doing my job and hateful threats followed, the resiliency I'd built as a runner helped me stand my ground and speak my truth back to the most powerful person in our country.

Building Resiliency with Daily Routines and Strong Foundations

Our ability to endure, to have hope for success despite any odds, is not automatic. But it is a muscle we can build. Running for me became a way to develop that habit of hope, of faith in myself that I can overcome hurdles and smash through barriers that circumstances might place in front of me. Whether I'm setting out to go 6 miles or 26.2, putting one foot in front of the other and getting it done, day in and day out, instills in my brain a reflex that I can do the same in other aspects of my life as well.

Whether you run or commit to some other daily physical or mental challenge, you can build your own strength to push through life's most monumental obstacles, developing a practice of overcoming your own doubts and achieving regular, tangible goals. Maybe it's completing a weekly crossword puzzle or getting up the nerve to raise your hand in class every time you meet.

In addition to our regular routines, we can ground our resiliency and capacity to persevere in identifying foundational rocks that can ground us and strengthen us in turbulent times.

I find that grounding in my faith and my family.

I was raised by a Catholic mom and Presbyterian dad, attending Bible study and Presbyterian church during most Sundays and Catholic mass on holidays. I had a keen sense of religion, but my faith in God developed through personal prayer, bible study, and fellowship with those of different but similarly sincerely held faiths. Throughout my spiritual growth and study of Eastern and Western religions, I've found that a relationship with a higher power, whether that be God or Allah or Yahweh, can ground our own sense of purpose and mission with an understanding of our own self along with our universal humanity and connection to one another.

Now, as a mom of an incredibly bright, charming, and precocious son, I've consistently found inspiration in seeing the world through his eyes. From the moment I learned I was going to be a mom throughout my time raising him, I've found a greater peace and grounding in knowing that above all, my greatest purpose is to be his parent. The honor of being a guide for him through this world as he forms his own beliefs and sense of who he is and who he wants to be is the greatest honor of my life. Knowing that, combined with the unequivocal, unconditional nature of a mom's love, constantly reminds me that I can indeed pick myself up and keep on going against any other challenges life throws my way. Because no matter the challenge, I'm always going to have the blessing of being a mom to a great boy who will always be in my corner, just as I will be in his. Whether I fall, fail, lose, or err, at the end of the day I still get to be Aiden's mom. And the constancy of that truth, along with the love that comes with it, is all that one little person will ever need from me. I end every day telling him two things: I love him, and I'm so lucky to be his mom. Those are his unconditional constants, no matter what. And they are my constants as well.

These parts of my life—running, my faith, my family, my home in Michigan, and the loved ones who surround me—provide a solid grounding in who I am. When I risk going off course, they can provide a place to return to, where I can find hope and belief in myself, and embolden me to stand my ground and push forward through fear and doubt. And they combine to collectively remind me of who I am and who I want to be, providing daily experiences that reinforce that sense of purpose and focus.

My son's kindergarten teacher, Amber, once asked his class: "What makes you you?"

"Roller coasters!" said my fearless little boy, then four years old. "Cats!" Arianna, one of his young friends, chimed in.

"No one else in the entire universe is you!" exclaimed five-year-old Lia excitedly, to her entire class.

"That's right!" Amber said to little Lia. "No one else in the entire universe is you."

I repeat that same simple question back to you, fellow warrior. What makes you you? Your answer may not be as simple as my son's and his classmates'. It may not be as broad and foundational as my answer of my faith and family, or point to an activity as time-consuming as running. But find your own definition of "what makes you uniquely you." Then develop habits and practices that help you recenter and get back up when life knocks you down.

Every day, unexpected developments, from tragedies we may endure to the successes others may achieve, can distract us from living our most authentic lives. We make a near constant series of choices, big and small, about how to respond to those developments. It's our responses to those opportunities and challenges that define who we are—our path, our purpose, and our contributions to our world.

Make resilience and perseverance a "baked-in" part of your response. Then employ daily practices and lean on fundamental building blocks, like your faith or family, to strengthen your resolve and inspire you to keep going and rise to any challenge.

That's how we all can build a sustainable journey as purposeful warriors that will take us, step-by-step, one foot in front of the other, to our destination.

A Nation of Purposeful Warriors

Never doubt that a small group of thoughtful,
committed citizens can change the world;
indeed, it's the only thing that ever has.

—MARGARET MEAD[1]

What makes you a warrior?

My warrior origin story begins with my parents, who taught me at a young age that everyone needs to have a seat at the table and equal access to opportunity in our country if our educational system and our economy are going to function and flourish. I grew up watching my mom and dad band together with other teachers to push school administrators to give all their students the same support and resources. My time in Alabama made clear to me that our best chance for everyone to have an equal chance to succeed in our country is equal access to the ballot box. It also underscored the power we have as citizens to achieve real and lasting progress when we work together to seek a better future for everyone, and the dangers we invite when we focus only on our individual prosperity and don't also consider the collective good.

I've since spent a few decades in the trenches working to show that government can work well for everyone and fighting for a more inclusive, equitable, and fair society. Along the way I've missed opportunities, lost elections, became a mom, suffered through toxic work environments, and navigated unexpected career shifts and job offers. Through all the peaks and valleys, I've tried to keep my head above water while responding to unpredictable twists and turns and built a life defined by principles I'm proud of—service, courage, honesty, and strength.

My north star, with roots in my faith and grounded in family, is ensuring we live in an inclusive, fair society where we honor every voice, protect every vote, and recognize our common humanity.

As Michigan's secretary of state and chief election official for nearly a decade, I've spent every day adjusting and adapting to a host of unexpected challenges. Whether battling efforts to intentionally mislead citizens about their right to vote, pushing back against powerful people trying to interfere with the counting of valid ballots, or guarding against very real, direct, and violent threats to my life, I've learned who I am. I'm someone who stands up to bullies. I won't let anyone silence me or the voices of millions of citizens who deserve to be heard. And I will take on anyone, anytime, anywhere, who tries to stand in the way of American citizens' constitutionally guaranteed rights and freedoms.

Whatever our purpose as a warrior might be, whatever dream or goal we may choose to fight for, there will always be people who seek to diminish and discourage us. But they only win if they convince us to give up—on our mission, and on ourselves.

Thankfully, there is a light within us, and a path forward for each of us, to be authentic, powerful, joyful, purposeful warriors—no matter what life may bring.

What If We All Became Purposeful Warriors?

When one of us stands in our power and pushes forward in service to our vision and goals, we can move mountains. Imagine what a community, a country, a world full of purposeful warriors could do.

Imagine what can be done if we come together, collectively standing up for what's right for ourselves and those around us, and apply these nine steps on our paths:

1. **Show solidarity.** Stand up for others and embrace others' fights for fairness and dignity as your own.

2. **Call out bullies.** Speak truth to power, even if it means going rogue.

3. **Speak your truth.** Don't give anyone else the power to define who you are and what you can accomplish.

4. **Embrace challenges with grit and grace.** Activate your bravery muscle and exercise it with kindness and empathy.

5. **Commit to innovation and continuous improvement.** Approach every task with an innovative spirit, question

assumptions, and take what seems to be working just fine and make it extraordinary.

6. **Channel anger into action.** Take the fire that underlies pain and rage and transform it into action.

7. **Be mission driven.** Chase results, not accolades, and measure your impact through your effect on others' lives.

8. **Build your own board of directors.** Work to intentionally surround yourself with people who will support you, mentor you, and help you stay on your path.

9. **Never give up.** Practice strength, resilience, and perseverance, and see challenges as opportunities to grow stronger.

We don't have to look far to see what could happen if we all embrace these principles as individuals—and as communities. To quote Margaret Mead, there are examples throughout history of a small group of "thoughtful, committed citizens" who change the world. "Indeed," she tells us, "it's the only thing that ever has." Countless transformative stories, from the civil rights movement, the antiwar movement, and the women's movement in the United States, to the end of apartheid in South Africa, reinforce this truth.

We can find those examples all around us. I got a personal glimpse into that power—the real and unrivaled influence that citizens standing together in unity as purposeful warriors can generate—back in 2020, during one of the lowest moments of our battle to protect Michigan's election results that year.

In Michigan, our elections are finalized by a vote of each local county board of canvassers, who have a ministerial responsibility to review the procedures and vote tallies in their county to ensure they are accurate. The state board of canvassers then follows with a final vote to certify and make the results official.

On November 16, 2020, the day of the board of canvassers meeting in Wayne County, the county in which Detroit sits, we received word that President Trump was personally calling the commissioners to pressure and cajole them into not certifying.

I came home that day feeling completely discouraged and defeated. Even though there was no valid reason not to finalize the election results, there was little I could do in that moment to stop a sitting president from successfully pressuring this board to delay or block the finalization of accurate and legitimate election results.

Of course, if the commissioners voted not to certify, they'd be violating the law, and we were prepared to go to court to force certification at the local and state level, where we were confident we'd win. But blocking certification in Wayne County and pushing the issue to the courts would delay the finalization of Michigan's election results and create enough doubt and uncertainty to enable the Trump campaign to push Pennsylvania, which was voting to finalize its election results the next week, to perhaps delay its certification as well. And we knew other dominos would fall after that.

How could we overcome the pressure of the president of the United States on local and state officials? Were the facts and law not enough?

Then something I'll never forget happened.

Hundreds of citizens showed up to the meeting of the Wayne County Board of Canvassers that evening. One by one, over the course of several hours, each spoke up to remind the canvassers of their duty under the law to make sure their votes counted.

They stood firm, didn't flinch, and demanded that their votes be certified as required under the law. Their voices mattered. And they would be heard.

One by one, they stood up for themselves. Together, they stood up for their community. All of them stood up for democracy.

Their actions, their voices, and their passionate, truthful arguments to the commissioners worked. These determined citizens turned the tide. The Wayne County Board of Canvassers ultimately fulfilled its duty, followed the law, and certified the 2020 election results. As a result, the state of Michigan, despite all the efforts of a president of the United States to pressure officials otherwise, was able to ensure that the individual who won the most votes in Michigan's 2020 presidential election—Joe Biden—was rightfully awarded our state's electoral votes and, with them, the presidency.

Because of those citizens and their determination, what started as the lowest moment of the 2020 election became the most inspiring. Facts and the rule of law carried the day, and truth triumphed.

The voters won.

And together we forged another chapter of history where democracy prevailed—just as it had in 1965, when everyday citizens stood at the foot of the Edmund Pettus Bridge in Selma and marched forward to demand that those in power similarly fulfill the American promise of one person, one vote.

It was an inspiring capstone to a challenging time and a reminder that, while we can accomplish much as individual warriors, we can achieve much more when we work together.

We all have the spark within us to become purposeful warriors. As individuals fighting with focus and a plan, we can do tremendous things to advance our hopes, vision, and goals and define our future.

We see that spark in the stories of warriors who take on those who try to delegitimize their work, their voices, and their integrity. It's there in the stories of everyday heroes who fight to make their corner of the world a little bit more just. All around us we see people—in our families, our workplaces, and our communities—rejecting divisiveness and fear to uplift our common humanity.

And when we take that notion one step further, and collectively harness our power as a united team of purposeful warriors, we build a force for change that can move mountains. The magnitude of what we can accomplish grows exponentially when we join with others who are similarly committed to rising above the noise and living authentic and meaningful lives.

We can envision a community filled with purposeful warriors who stand up for themselves and each other, recognizing our commonalities, seeking truth, embracing discomfort, questioning assumptions, fighting with grace and grit, and never giving up.

As purposeful warriors we can—indeed, must—use that spirit to define what comes next. And together we can forge a collective, prosperous, united path alongside others who choose to be purposeful warriors too.

We can all choose to respond to twists and turns and stand, undeterred, at the foot of the metaphorical Edmund Pettus Bridge. Just as in 1965, and just as in 2020, wherever there are serious and real threats to rights and freedoms, to the values of inclusion, respect, fairness, and equality that our country was founded upon, we can be the ones to lead the way out of the abyss.

We have the power to decide the future of our nation.

We have the power to make sure that our kids are safe and can go to school free from fear of gun violence, that women will have control over their own bodies, and that we all will have clean air to breathe and clean water to drink.

We have the power to ensure that the freedom to vote—our democracy—will remain secure.

Actualizing that power means working together to push ahead in service of who we are, the rights we stand for, and the values and community we seek to protect. One where democracy thrives and justice prevails. One where different perspectives and mutual respect are valued. A society that is inclusive, fair, filled with warriors who honor every voice and revel in our common humanity.

That is the world I am fighting for. That is the world the stories and experiences shared throughout this book can embolden us all to fight for. And that is the world that, fighting together as purposeful warriors, we all can build together.

I hope that you'll join me.

Acknowledgments

This book would not exist without the support, advice, and insights of many friends and colleagues who helped bring it to fruition over the course of several years. Here are a few who went to particularly crucial lengths to make *The Purposeful Warrior* a reality.

I started writing in February 2021. As a witness to an historic election cycle in 2020—buttressed by a global pandemic and an unprecedented, coordinated effort to deny and overturn the will of the voters—so much of what we experienced in Michigan throughout 2020 was at that time still an untold story. I am indebted to Teri Steinberg, who helped me talk through my experiences and begin to explore whether there was a "book in there." We soon found there was much more to share than those events, and our conversations grew into collaborations with another friend and trusted adviser, Rafe Sagalyn. Rafe read many, many draft outlines and proposals that took several forms over the course of three years. His feedback was invaluable as I worked to shape a series of stories and insights into a unique and readable tome.

I'm deeply grateful to Matthew Dowd for generously providing so much support, advice, and even a space to write when I needed it—all of which helped me begin drafting chapters and working through ideas for the book's call to action. Matthew's experience writing books that are equal parts political memoir and personal advice helped me begin trying to tell my own story in a way that is authentic and helpful, I hope, to others.

These pages never would have seen the light of day had Matt Littman and Mara Freedman not met me for brunch and somehow decided I should meet Maria Shriver, and quickly made the introduction that led to this book being in your hands.

From the moment I met Maria over coffee in Los Angeles in November 2023 I knew my book had found a home with someone whose sincere vision, drive, sense of service, and commitment to motivating others is beautiful, rare, and inspirational. For over an hour we discussed our lives as she grilled me with insightful questions and offered perceptive advice. After we met I immediately knew anything I wanted to write—and publish—would be made better through Maria's mentoring, guidance, and devotion to sharing and amplifying the same kinds of stories I wanted to tell.

From there my friends at Dupree Miller—particularly the incomparable Jan Miller and Shannon Marven—went to work. I soon found myself in trustworthy and deeply thoughtful hands with the Penguin Random House and Open Field team. Thank you, Brian Tart and Nina Rodriguez-Marty, for embracing this book with such enthusiasm, and the brilliant Cassidy Graham for holding my hand throughout the editing process as we worked to take *The Purposeful Warrior* to another level of precision and clarity. You all made this book readable, and I am forever grateful for your time, patience, and help staying on deadline.

I am thankful to so many friends from different moments of my life for reading through earlier drafts and helping sift through potential book covers. Amanda Seyfried and Tommy Sadoski, Andrea Kovach, Sean Braswell, Melissa Coulier, Lisa Lis, Sheri Mark, Heaster Wheeler, Jake Rollow, Winnie Liao, Melanie Elturk, and Ronja Bandyopadhyay offered repeated, patient, and honest takes in response to my incessant texts and emails with new versions asking, "What about this?" Topping this list is my extraordinary special and dear friend Caitlin McHugh Stamos, who offered particularly critical, very well-informed, and unflinching advice when I needed it most.

Finally, to my family: you made this possible. Thank you, Ryan Friedrichs, for being my partner in parenting our bright and precocious son. I never would have completed this book without your support (and well-timed distractions for Aiden). Your years of unconditional love and support have made me a better person and I hope with this book more people can know of your unrivaled commitment to honesty, integrity, and loyalty. And to Aiden Benson Friedrichs, your joy, humor, kindness, bravery, and sense of adventure is unrivaled. Being your mom is the greatest honor of my life. I love you to the moon and back.

Notes

INTRODUCTION

1. Chögyam Trungpa, *Shambhala: The Sacred Path of the Warrior* (Shambhala Publications, 1984), 65.
2. "Statement from Secretary of State Jocelyn Benson Concerning Threats against Her and Her Family," Dec. 6, 2020, michigan.gov/sos/resources/news/2020/12/06/statement-from-secretary-of-state-jocelyn-benson-concerning-threats-against-her-and-her-family.
3. David Eggert, "Record 5.5M Voted in Michigan; Highest Percentage in Decades," Associated Press, Nov. 5, 2020, apnews.com/article/record-votes-michigan-highest-turnout-1f7802d2a2e67966ba8ccb02e3d1cbed.
4. Mary Oliver, "The Summer Day," in *House of Light* (Beacon Press, 1990).

CHAPTER 1

1. Robert F. Kennedy, Day of Affirmation Address, delivered at the University of Cape Town, South Africa, June 6, 1966, jfklibrary.org/learn/about-jfk/the-kennedy-family/robert-f-kennedy/robert-f-kennedy-speeches/day-of-affirmation-address-university-of-capetown-capetown-south-africa-june-6-1966.
2. Taken from a detailed account of Liuzzo's experience by her daughter Sally Liuzzo-Prado, in Karen Grigsby Bates, "Killed for Taking Part in 'Everybody's Fight,'" *All Things Considered*, NPR, Aug. 18, 2013, npr.org/2013/08/18/213266280/viola-liuzzo-a-white-martyr-in-the-civil-rights-movement.
3. "Dissertations, On Government," In *The Life and Works of Thomas Paine*, ed. W. Van der Wede from *Thomas Paine Friends Bulletin* 9, no. 3, (2008): thomaspaine.us/studyguide_res_publica.html.
4. Viola Liuzzo, untitled poem, published with written permission of her daughter Mary Liuzzo.
5. Donna Britt, "A White Mother Went to Alabama to Fight for Civil Rights. The Klan Killed Her for It," *Washington Post*, Dec. 15, 2017, washingtonpost

.com/news/retropolis/wp/2017/12/15/a-white-mother-went-to-alabama-to-fight
-for-civil-rights-the-klan-killed-her-for-it/.

6. Lyndon B. Johnson, "Address to Congress—We Shall Overcome, 1965," Mar. 15, 1965, pbs.org/wgbh/americanexperience/features/lbj-overcome.

7. Author's interview with Mary Liuzzo, Mar. 2, 2022.

8. The research department regularly published its findings in the Intelligence Project, past issues of which are available at splcenter.org/intelligence-report.

9. Southern Poverty Law Center, "Hyman Greenbaum's Son Hard at Work with Neo-Nazi Group," *Intelligence Report*, June 15, 1999, splcenter.org/fighting-hate /intelligence-report/1999/hyman-greenbaum's-son-hard-work-neo-nazi-group.

CHAPTER 2

1. William Faulkner, speech delivered to the graduating class of University of Mississippi, May 28, 1951, americanrhetoric.com/MovieSpeeches/moviespeechwilliam faulknerofoxford.html.

2. *Davis v. Benson*, Michigan Court of Appeals, Sept. 2020, michigan.gov/ag/-/me dia/Project/Websites/AG/releases/2020/september/COA_354622_ROBERT _DAVIS_V_SECRETARY_OF_STATE_Opinion_-_Authored_-_Published _09162020_702488_7.pdf.

3. Heather Cox Richardson, "Mr Trump: My Name Is Jocelyn Benson." May 21, 2020, thehobbledehoy.com/2020/05/21/mr-trump-my-name-is-jocelyn-benson/.

4. Jocelyn Benson, Election Night Press Conference, youtube.com/watch?v=hA AnWZFQm64.

5. Tim Alberta, "The Michigan Republican Who Stopped Trump," *Politico*, Nov. 24, 2020, politico.com/newsletters/politico-nightly/2020/11/24/the-michigan-republican -who-stopped-trump-490984.

6. Alberta, "The Michigan Republican Who Stopped Trump."

7. "Read the Full Transcript and Listen to Trump's Audio Call with Georgia Secretary of State," CNN, Jan. 3, 2021, cnn.com/2021/01/03/politics/trump-brad -raffensperger-phone-call-transcript/index.html.

8. Donald J. Trump (@RealDonaldTrump), "I spoke to Secretary of State Brad Raffensperger yesterday about Fulton County and voter fraud in Georgia. He was unwilling, or unable, to answer questions such as the 'ballots under table' scam . . . ," Twitter, Jan. 3, 2021, 8:57 a.m., x.com/realDonaldTrump/status/134573104386 1659650.

9. Secretary Brad Raffensperger (@GASecofState), "Respectfully, President Trump: What you're saying is not true. The truth will come out," Twitter, Jan. 3, 2021, 10:27 a.m., x.com/GaSecofState/status/1345753643593687040.

10. Linda So, "Trump-Inspired Death Threats Are Terrorizing Election Workers," June 11, 2021, reuters.com/investigates/special-report/usa-trump-georgia-threats/.

11. So, "Trump-Inspired Death Threats Are Terrorizing Election Workers."

12. Sam Levine, "He Became a Hero for Halting Trump's Efforts to Overturn the Election. Will Voters Now Punish Him?," *The Guardian*, May 19, 2022, the guardian.com/us-news/2022/may/19/georgia-brad-raffensperger-trump-election -secretary-state.

13. Martin Pengelly, "'There's Nowhere I Feel Safe': Georgia Election Workers on How Trump Upended Their Lives," *The Guardian*, June 21, 2022, theguardian .com/us-news/2022/jun/21/january-6-hearings-georgia-elections-workers-mother -daughter-testify.
14. Elie Wiesel, "Hope, Despair and Memory," Nobel Lecture, December 11, 1986, nobelprize.org/prizes/peace/1986/wiesel/lecture/.

CHAPTER 3

1. Edwards, Gareth, dir. *Rogue One: A Star Wars Story.* United States: Lucasfilm, Ltd., 2016.
2. Thurston Clarke, *The Last Campaign: Robert F. Kennedy and 82 Days That Inspired America* (Henry Holt, 2008).
3. Clarke, *The Last Campaign*, 189.
4. Clarke, *The Last Campaign*, 190.
5. Clarke, *The Last Campaign*, 190.
6. Clarke, *The Last Campaign*, 190.
7. Clarke, *The Last Campaign*, 190.
8. Clarke, *The Last Campaign*, 190.
9. Clarke, *The Last Campaign*, 189.
10. Clarke, *The Last Campaign*, 281.
11. Clarke, *The Last Campaign*, 281.
12. Jennifer Kennedy, "Wayne Law Continues Remarkable Rise in Latest U.S. News & World Report Rankings," April 9, 2024, law.wayne.edu/news/wayne-law-continues -remarkable-rise-in-latest-us-news-world-report-rankings-61986.

CHAPTER 4

1. Audre Lorde, *The Cancer Journals* (Aunt Lute Books, 1980), 8.
2. Governor Gretchen Whitmer, "Governor Whitmer Delivers Prepared Remarks Prepared Remarks on Law Enforcement Operation," press release, Oct. 8, 2020, michigan .gov/whitmer/news/press-releases/2020/10/08/governor-whitmer-delivers-prepared -remarks-prepared-remarks-on-law-enforcement-operation.

CHAPTER 5

1. David Maraniss, *When Pride Still Mattered: A Life of Vince Lombardi* (Simon & Schuster, 1999), 458.
2. Saskia Sorrosa, "If It Ain't Broke, Fix It Anyway," *Medium*, Aug. 9, 2018, medium .com/@ssorrosa/if-it-aint-broke-fix-it-anyway-5fccbe4f2d00.
3. Vivian Nunez, "From NBA Executive to Food Entrepreneur: How This Latina Built Her Dream Company," *Forbes*, Oct. 25, 2017, forbes.com/sites/viviannunez /2017/10/25/from-nba-executive-to-food-entrepreneur-how-this-latina-built-her -dream-company/?sh=54cd412f7828.
4. Chantelle Bacigalupo, "Four Business Tips from an NBA Executive Turned Entrepreneur," *We All Grow* (blog), undated, weallgrowlatina.com/4-business-tips -from-an-nba-executive-turned-entrepreneur/.
5. Bacigalupo, "Four Business Tips."

CHAPTER 6

1. Michelle Obama, Interview with Stephen Colbert, *The Late Show with Stephen Colbert*, Nov. 14, 2022, youtube.com/watch?v=8gfqh-ZrHY8 at 16:56.
2. Todd Ouida Obituary, *Penn Live Patriot-News*, Sept. 25, 2001, https://obits.penn live.com/us/obituaries/pennlive/name/todd-ouida-obituary?pid=98376.
3. President Barack Obama, "The New Way Forward," speech, U.S. Military Academy, West Point, NY, Dec. 1, 2009, obamawhitehouse.archives.gov/blog/2009/12/01/new-way-forward-presidents-address.
4. Air Force Captain Joel Gentz, American Fallen Heroes Project, thefallen.militarytimes.com/air-force-1st-lt-joel-c-gentz/4667056.
5. Army Pfc. Shane Cantu, Honor the Fallen, thefallen.militarytimes.com/army-pfc-shane-w-cantu/6568333.
6. For a full review of the 2000 election controversy in Florida, see Jeffrey Toobin, *Too Close to Call: The Thirty-Six Day Battle to Decide the 2000 Election* (UK: Random House Publishing Group, 2001).
7. Martin Kettle, "Florida 'Recounts' Make Gore Winner," *The Guardian*, Jan. 29, 2001, theguardian.com/world/2001/jan/29/uselections2000.usa.
8. President George W. Bush inaugural address, delivered Jan. 21, 2001, georgewbush-whitehouse.archives.gov/news/inaugural-address.html.

CHAPTER 7

1. Nelson Mandela, "Address by Nelson Mandela during the 90th Birthday Celebration of Mr Walter Sisulu," Walter Sisulu Hall, Randburg, Johannesburg, South Africa, May 18, 2002, mandela.gov.za/mandela_speeches/2002/020518_sisulu.htm.
2. Loren Eiseley, "The Starfish Story," in *The Unexpected Universe* (Harcourt, Brace and World, 1969), 48–66.
3. Amy Gill, "Remembering Judge Damon Keith," *The Detroit Jewish News*, May 7, 2019, updated July 10, 2023, thejewishnews.com/news/local/remembering-judge-damon-keith/article_ea2a724f-ebe2-54f5-b93c-60491a54b935.html.
4. Peter Gould, "Building Purposeful Teams: Melanie Elturk," peter-gould.com/interviews/building-purposeful-teams.

CHAPTER 8

1. Kathleen Gray, "Trump vs. the Women Who Lead Michigan: A Battle with 2020 Implications," *The New York Times,* July 12, 2020, nytimes.com/2020/07/12/us/politics/trump-michigan-whitmer-benson-nessel.html.
2. Benjamin Wallace-Wells, "How Gretchen Whitmer Made Michigan a Democratic Stronghold," *The New Yorker*, July 24, 2023, newyorker.com/magazine/2023/07/24/how-gretchen-whitmer-made-michigan-a-democratic-stronghold.
3. Oralandar Brand-Williams, "Same-Sex Case Lawyer to Run for Mich. Attorney General," *The Detroit News*, Aug. 15, 2017, detroitnews.com/story/news/politics/2017/08/15/dana-nessel-michigan-attorney-general/104615126/.
4. Under the state of Michigan constitution, party nominees for secretary of state and attorney general are chosen by Michigan democratic party members who at-

tend the state convention. See Michigan State Constitution, Section 21, "The lieutenant governor, secretary of state and attorney general shall be nominated by party conventions in a manner prescribed by law," Const. 1963, Art. V, § 21, Eff. Jan. 1, 1964.

5. "Putting an End to Sexual Harassment Scandals," YouTube, Nov. 27, 2017, youtube.com/watch?v=CQL37wcgI6k.

6. Samantha Ettus, "Dana Nessel Is Running for Office and Hitting Them Where It Hurts," *Forbes*, Dec. 1, 2017, forbes.com/sites/samanthaettus/2017/12/01/shes runningforoffice/.

7. Dana Nessel, "One day, because of Governor Gretchen Whitmer's emergency orders, there will be thousands of people who would have otherwise died who instead will go on to watch their kids graduate from school, have grandchildren . . ." Facebook, Apr. 11, 2020, facebook.com/DanaNesselAG/posts/255565565143 0093/.

8. Danielle Bayard Jackson, *Fighting for Our Friendships: The Science and Art of Conflict and Connection in Women's Relationships* (Hachette Books, 2024), 24.

9. "Remarks by President Trump, Vice President Pence, and Members of the Coronavirus Task Force in Press Briefing," The White House, Mar. 28, 2020, trump whitehouse.archives.gov/briefings-statements/remarks-president-trump-vice -president-pence-members-coronavirus-task-force-press-briefing-13/.

10. President Donald J. Trump (@RealDonaldTrump), "The Wacky Do Nothing Attorney General of Michigan, Dana Nessel, is viciously threatening Ford Motor Company for the fact that I inspected a Ventilator plant without a mask," Twitter, May 21, 2020, 11:14 p.m., x.com/realDonaldTrump/status/12636694333667 28704.

11. Gray, "Trump vs. the Women Who Lead Michigan: A Battle With 2020 Implications."

12. Jocelyn Benson (@JocelynBenson), "We ready," Twitter, Nov. 7, 2022, 9:22 p.m., x.com/JocelynBenson/status/1589805404426567680.

13. Jan Torrisi-Mokwa, *Building Career Equity* (Congruence Press, 2016), 76.

14. Melissa Eisler, "Your Own Personal Board of Directors," Wide Lens Leadership, June 6, 2022, widelensleadership.com/your-personal-board-of-directors/.

CHAPTER 9

1. Winston Churchill, "Address at Harrow School: Never Give In," Oct. 29, 1941, academyatthelakes.org/wp-content/uploads/2016/02/WSChurchillNeverGiveIn Excerpts.pdf.

CONCLUSION

1. Margaret Mead, *The World Ahead: An Anthropologist Anticipates the Future*, ed. Robert B. Textor (Berghahn Books, 2005), 12.